Penguin

Buying a

Lesley Vickers spent several years [...] Law Courts and is an authority on now to go from Fleet Street to Carey Street without getting wet. She is now the senior partner of a firm of solicitors in London and an experienced broadcaster on legal subjects. She and her family have been involved in many moves during the last few years – this book is based on their experiences as well as that of her many clients.

L. E. Vickers

Buying a House or Flat

Third Edition

Penguin Books

Penguin Books Ltd, Harmondsworth, Middlesex, England
Viking Penguin Inc., 40 West 23rd Street, New York, New York 10010, U.S.A.
Penguin Books Australia Ltd, Ringwood, Victoria, Australia
Penguin Books Canada Ltd, 2801 John Street, Markham, Ontario, Canada L3R 1B4
Penguin Books (N.Z.) Ltd, 182–190 Wairau Road, Auckland 10, New Zealand

First published as *Buying a House* 1970
Reprinted with revisions 1972, 1974, 1975, 1976
Revised and reissued under the present title 1977
Reprinted with revisions 1979, 1980
Second edition 1981
Third edition 1985

Made and printed in Great Britain by
Richard Clay (The Chaucer Press) Ltd
Bungay, Suffolk
Filmset in Monophoto Photina by
Northumberland Press Ltd, Gateshead
Tyne and Wear

Warning

This book explains what experts are doing: it is not a do-it-yourself book. Neither the publishers nor the author accept responsibility for loss arising, through whatever cause, from anything written in this book.

The law and practice described are those of England and Wales, and may be different in Scotland.

To Chris, Chris, Chrissy and Kirsten.
Likewise to Julie, Peter,
Alex, Laura and Michael,
with thanks for keeping me on the move.

Contents

Acknowledgements   8
Introduction   9

Part 1: The Search

1   Mainly for First-Time Buyers   13
2   Where to Look for Your House   21
3   Where Will the Money Come From?   34
4   The Cost of Buying and Running a House   57
5   Estate Agents   75

Part 2: The House You Want

6   Meeting the Owner and Making Sure   83
7   Help! You Need a Solicitor   92
8   The Deposit   99
9   Surveyors   106
10 Buying a Flat or a New House   111
11 Other Possibilities   122

Part 3: Why It Takes So Long

12 Solicitors' Work Before Contract   131
13 Between Contract and Completion   142
14 Preparing Your Move   156

Glossary   171
Index   173

Acknowledgements

I am most grateful to the Chief Land Registrar for allowing me the use of facsimile copies of entries of the Land Register, and to the Town Clerks of Ealing and Camden for information about the working of the Land Charges Departments. My thanks also go to my husband, to many friends who helped with the present edition, and to my clients who obligingly buy houses in all parts of the country.

Introduction

Since the last edition of this book politics have crept into house-buying. The promise of cheaper conveyancing costs is tempting to a nation of houseowners. The problem is how to provide cheaply the expertise for which solicitors sweat in some of the most difficult professional examinations and with years of practical training. The answer has not quite been found. It is not likely to come from computers, which turn out beautifully printed documents but cannot think. In the meantime some firms of solicitors are cutting prices; also a new semi-qualification has been invented. Interesting projects are being tried out – many with the aim of giving the housebuyer details of houses, mortgages, insurance and legal adbice, all under one roof.

Please remember – you should not have to pay anything beyond:

(1)   a valuation fee to the building society or bank who lends you the money;

(2)   legal fees to the solicitor who gets you the house;

(3)   to the state: VAT, search fees, stamp duty (if the house costs over £30,000), and possibly Land Registry fees.

The last item is often the most costly and consists mainly of tax, a fact which receives little publicity. Remember also that you do not normally have to pay estate agents or brokers. You should not be forced into buying insurance which you do not require.

This book is written to stop you from paying more than you need, help you get proper advice at the proper time, and help you get value for money.

JANUARY 1985

Part I

The Search

Chapter 1

Mainly for First-Time Buyers

Unless you have large savings, win the pools or inherit a great deal of money, you are unlikely to be buying your first – or quite possibly your second or third – house for cash. Fortunately you ought to be able to borrow the bulk of the price on mortgage.

Therefore, start by finding out from one or two building societies how much money they will let you borrow, and on what type of house. Your income determines how much the building society may be willing to lend you. The age and type of building determines what percentage of the price of the house this loan can be. You may be able to borrow 90 per cent of the cost of a new or nearly new house, but probably not of a Victorian flat.

Next, add to the possible mortgage the amount of your savings, take at least £1,000–£2,000 off the total for removal, furnishing, etc. and you are left with a figure which gives an approximate idea of how much you can spend on a house. You are now well placed to look at properties in your preferred price range, without wasting an inordinate amount of time. Spend some of the time saved by reading the chapters in this book aimed at helping you to find a house within your means and avoiding disaster.

To illustrate some of the problems and pitfalls waiting to trap first-time buyers, let us follow the fortunes of three friends who shared a rented flat. They woke one morning realizing that spring had come and that everyone seemed to be house-hunting. They joined the throng and in their modest way added to the spring fever which seems to sweep the nation every now and then and results in disproportionate price increases. If buyers kept calm while the daffodils were in bloom, a manic rise such as that of 1978/9 might abate more quickly.

Our friends soon realized that buying a house was rather more involved than buying a car. Their lives were pleasant, their savings small. They did not have enough money. Bella, who had a weight problem, decided to lay the foundation for her housing fund by cutting out sweets and biscuits. Every time she felt the urge for carbohydrates, she put 10p into a special purse. May gave up smoking and put by the price of a packet of cigarettes twice a day. At the end of two months Bella fitted into size 10, May complained of putting on weight, and their savings, though greater than they had been, remained distinctly modest.

Jack put all his loose change in a beer mug at the end of each day. Apart from crises, such as no money for gas or one of the girls running out of cigarettes or sweets, his savings rose visibly. Nevertheless, all three soon came to the conclusion that saving alone was not going to enable them to buy a house.

The next step, therefore, was for them to take weekend jobs and to put aside a percentage of their earnings. After a few months they saw that even at this rate of self-denial it would take them years to buy. They therefore thought they might club together. Rather than aim at buying three separate houses, they would try to buy one flat between them. The first step in this direction was for each of them to don their most respectable clothes and to visit a building society. Each went to a different society and in the evening they compared experiences.

None of them came back with a firm promise of money for a flat. All three had a better idea of what they could aim at and which society was likely to be most useful to them. On one point all building societies were agreed: three people might be allowed to buy together, but the maximum amount they could borrow would be calculated on the income of one, or at best two, of them. 'Think what would happen if one of you wanted to leave. You might not find a replacement and the mortgage would still have to be paid every month' was the kind of fatherly comment they met. The same argument did not apply to the suggestion which they tried out on one or two societies: that Jack and one of the girls should buy together. The fatherly building society manager was prepared to treat them as fiancés and to lend on both incomes.

May, who as a teacher commanded a respectable settled income, was told she could count on borrowing 2·5 to 2·75 times her annual income on a house approved by the society. The society was also willing to add the equivalent of Jack's income to the loan. May needed to have a savings account with the society for at least six months before buying. Such delays or conditions are imposed every now and then, but are not inevitable. Building societies have found no way of ensuring a steady supply of funds into their coffers and are therefore quickly affected by the state of both the housing market and the stock market. There is nothing the individual borrower can do about this, except, perhaps, to keep money in two different societies.

Bella's income was going up by leaps and bounds. She lived as comfortably as May. In the eyes of the building society, however, she was a less attractive borrower. Her work was that of a freelance researcher: as with all self-employed persons, building societies want to see two or three years' accounts, preferably audited or accepted by the Tax Inspector. Bella sensed that the manager doubted her business abilities. He had clearly failed to realize the quality of person he was dealing with. Within two weeks Bella had prepared detailed accounts, collected her bank statements and obtained a number of firm contracts for her work. Her earnings for the current year promised to be far better than last year's. The building society manager was unimpressed. Bella contacted mortgage brokers and found that she could borrow through them what she needed, but that it would cost more than a simple building society repayment mortgage. She worked out that the best purchase for her was a converted flat, i.e. part of what used to be a one-family house. The brokers could negotiate a mortgage for part of the money with a building society of their choice. That loan would be based on her income for the last tax year. There would be a second mortgage, at a higher rate of interest, to bring the total loan to 75 per cent of the price of the flat. She would be compelled to secure both mortgages by insurance policies – this was the condition exacted by the brokers whose business was the selling of life insurance.

By committing herself to unusually high outgoings, Bella might achieve her aim of buying a flat without waiting till she had three years' accounts with which to dazzle a building society. She realized that if she were unlucky she might pay a broker's fee yet not get all the money she needed. Under the provisions of the Consumer Credit Act 1974 brokers are not entitled to more than £1 unless you obtain a mortgage within six months, but in practice it is not always easy to get back the balance of the broker's fee.

Bella argued that house prices would continue to rise and that she would do better with a flat than without.

Anyone whose income is high enough to afford large mortgage payments but who cannot get a building society to recognize this, may find it worthwhile to approach brokers to see whether they can get a more generous loan. Self-employed people, recent arrivals from overseas, people with fluctuating incomes or who rely heavily on overtime pay are among those who sometimes have this problem. But always try the ordinary sources first (see Chapter 3): they will almost certainly be cheaper.

Jack worked out that house prices were likely to level out in the autumn. By then he would have saved some more money and would be able to choose carefully and to buy at leisure. He realized that his first flat was to be the currency with which to buy all future homes. If he bought wisely, his flat would go up in value and would allow him to buy a better home next time. His building society, when told he wanted to buy together with May, was agreeable, but flatly refused to treat her income as the main one on which to calculate its loan. They offered two and a half times Jack's low trainee income plus a third of May's as a teacher. Building societies have a good deal of discretion, hence the wisdom of investing your savings with more than one.

One of the plans considered, but eventually discarded, was for one of them to join up with another friend, Libby. Libby was in the throes of a divorce. She had two children and, with her husband, owned a house in London. Bitter battles had been fought; Libby was now picking up the pieces and working out plans for the future. The house would be sold, the children would live with her and she would get enough money from the sale for a modest home away from London. She had considered the alternative of buying a larger house with Roger, her ex-husband. Roger was willing to wait for his share of the proceeds from the house till the children had left school. Libby did not warm to the idea of having to move house again at Roger's bidding, nor of having to rely on him for regular contributions to her outgoings on the new house. She decided on independence in the country and also against buying a new home with one of her friends, although her capital and their earnings would have enabled them to buy quite a good house.

Our friends decided to go their separate ways. Bella pushed ahead, confident that she could cope with exceptionally high monthly payments. Jack completed his training, then bought a flat in Dragon Court (see Chapter 10, 'Buying a Flat or a New House'). May married Tom Jones: we shall meet her again.

Reminders – Particularly for First-Time Buyers

Budget
Read Chapter 4, 'The Cost of Buying and Running a House'. Don't buy a house you can't afford to run, but remember:

monthly mortgage payments are unlikely to rise as much as your income, even if interest rates should go up;

the value of your house will almost certainly go up over the years. Your mortgage debt won't. If you are unlucky, lose your leg or your livelihood, and have to rely on social security, the DHSS will almost certainly help with mortgage payments too;

your mortgage payments will not cost as much as you think, because of tax relief.

Plan Ahead
Unless you have a lot of money available, you cannot buy a house on the spur of the moment. You will probably need:

a minimum of 11–12 per cent of the purchase price of the house, to allow for the deposit and the expenses connected with buying. If your income is low and you cannot get a high mortgage, you may well need a higher percentage;

an annual income of nearly half the amount you want to borrow from a building society.

More about both these points in Chapters 3 and 4.

You would do well to put your savings into one or more building societies and to get some idea of how much you can borrow before you start serious house-hunting.

There are, of course, exceptions:

a sitting tenant may well be able to get a 100 per cent mortgage to buy a house at a favourable rate;

a council tenant may be able to buy his house with a 100 per cent mortgage and at a much reduced price;

the employees of banks and building societies or of some large companies can often get mortgages at favourable rates.

These are not instant solutions to your problem. Cheap loans, or 100 per cent loans, do not tend to be available to newcomers.

Raising Money

If you are buying at a time when mortgages are hard to come by:

check your prospects with your building society. If they are poor, consider moving your savings;

see whether an estate agent or your solicitor can suggest a building society;

try to buy a house on a new estate offering mortgages to buyers (see magazines such as *Housebuyer* for suitable advertisements);

if you can afford higher monthly payments but initially cannot borrow sufficient funds from a building society or local authority, try a mortgage broker. Brokers often arrange mortgages at higher than normal cost.

At a time when mortgages are plentiful you may want to shop around. Building societies, though they apply the same general rules, vary in many details, e.g. how they calculate your income; what proportion of a second income they will take into account; the maximum sum they will lend on one house; the rate of interest charged on an endowment mortgage. More about this in Chapter 3.

Choosing a House

Read Chapters 2 and 6, 'Where to Look for Your House' and 'Meeting the Owner and Making Sure'.

Parting with Money

Estate agents do not charge a fee to house-hunters. You may, however, be asked to pay a deposit on the house of your choice. Before paying, read Chapters 6 and 8, 'Meeting the Owner and Making Sure' and 'The Deposit', and never pay a deposit direct to the house-owner. Having made an offer, the only other fee you should have to pay before proceeding further is the building society's inspection fee, which is based on the price of the house.

General

If prices have kept fairly steady during the last year there is a good chance that they will jump next spring. It is therefore worth considering whether you can buy in winter. However, if prices rose sharply in the spring, the rise will probably have tailed off by late summer.

If you do have to buy at a time of rapidly rising prices, there may well be a rush for houses which can become a panic. In order to stand the best chance, therefore, of finding what you want you must:

have 10–15 per cent of the price of the house, preferably in a building society;

have an agreement in principle from that building society for a loan of £x thousand;

know what kind of house you can afford and where;

buy early editions of newspapers advertising such houses;

regularly telephone estate agents handling such houses, and make sure they have a telephone number where they can reach you, or a member of your family, during the day.

You may have to make up your mind very quickly, or someone else will buy before you. At such a time you may prefer to buy without all the careful investigations and preparations recommended in this book on the principle of 'better a pig in a poke than no pig at all'. Whatever you take on trust, do stick out for four sound walls and, if possible, a sound roof. The cost of replacing a roof may be greater than the rise in prices between this year and next. Also, before embarking on each step, read as much of this book as you can, making a point to look particularly carefully at the first aid Chapters 7 and 8, 'Help! You Need a Solicitor' and 'The Deposit'.

However, even if everything goes more or less to plan, resign yourself: it could well take six months from the time you find the house to the time you move in. Also, do prepare for possible disappointment: you may not buy this particular house, either because you can't raise enough money, or get a bad report on its structural condition, or don't like it so much on your second visit, or decide you can't afford it, or your seller has a similar problem with the house he is thinking of buying. A sizeable number of people do not end up with the house they first intend buying.

You may well be wondering by now whether all the effort and anxiety are worth taking on. The answer probably is: yes. Quite apart from the fact that you need somewhere to live, a house, carefully chosen, becomes a useful commodity and in all likelihood gives your financial position an uplift. House prices have over a number of years either kept up with inflation or moved up faster than other prices. Once you have a house, this rise need not worry you, as your own property should keep step and make buying the next very much easier than the first.

Chapter 2

Where to Look for Your House

I had my first taste of house-hunting at the age of eleven, when my uncle, a writer, announced that he needed quiet surroundings for his work. My aunt and I spent the best part of that summer poring over Ordnance Survey maps and travelling along the country lanes of Scotland, Derbyshire, Devon and Wales. Country life, in however remote a spot, we found to include a great deal of barking, braying, crowing, hooting or whistling, none of which could be tolerated by my uncle. He therefore moved to a flat in Manchester, where noise was continuous and anonymous and where he wrote some of his most interesting books.

Like my uncle, Libby, who had recently been divorced, could choose to live anywhere in the country. Such a wide choice can be difficult. One of Libby's friends had carefully selected a district particularly awkward to reach from her ex-husband's home. She was defeated by the advent of a motorway. Libby had been able to make a clean break when the marriage came to grief. She received a sum of money from the sale of the old house and intended using it for a new home for herself and the children, who were still below school age.

She drew up a rough list of her requirements:

Libby's first list
At least four rooms
Small town (she thought this would give her the best chance of finding reasonable schools for the children and part-time work for herself).

Clearly, before Libby could seriously start house-hunting, she needed to be more precise and to decide on one or two areas in which to concentrate her search.

Should your choice be as wide as Libby's, start by deciding

roughly what kind of house you would like – town or country, old or new – and then buy a paper such as *Dalton's Weekly* or *Country Life* (depending on your purse and preference). You will get an idea of where you can find your kind of house at your kind of price. Bear in mind that house prices vary extraordinarily, often for reasons unconnected with the building: they are higher near town centres, in south-east England, in areas of full employment, in country areas easily reached from a big city.

For most house-buyers the initial search is easier and more precise. They know roughly where they want to live: near their job, relatives, children's school, or whatever else may be particularly important to them.

Take, for example, Tom and May Jones, recently married. They have put their savings into two building societies. Tom is in his first job and intends to move on after about two years. May, as a teacher, is fairly mobile. One society is prepared to lend twice May's income plus half of Tom's; the other refuses to treat a wife's income as the major one and would give them only two and a half times Tom's annual income, as the main breadwinner, plus one third of May's. The difference is some £2,000. Tom and May need a home which is easy to run, easy to sell when the time comes, and for which a large deposit will not be required. They want to spend as little time as possible on travelling to and from work, so they take out a map and start writing.

Tom and May's first list
Area – radius of five miles from work
Price – up to £x thousand
Accommodation – modern, i.e. built since 1960, minimum three rooms.

Peter is hoping for promotion. He would like to try for a job in London and expects to sell his very pleasant house in the Midlands at a good profit. His wife works part-time and they have three children.

Peter's first list
Area – London
Price up to £x thousand
Accommodation – minimum eight rooms.

Your First List

It is as well not to go into too much detail with this first list, and to start finding out what kind of house can be had at what price in the chosen area. Four or five main points are quite enough.

How do you go about finding out? House-hunting is best done in two parts; part one can be usefully carried out from the depth of your armchair, with an occasional stroll to your newsagent or to the public library. It is worth spending a good deal of time and some money on this part of the hunt, particularly if you are moving to a part of the country which is new to you. A few pounds spent on newspapers, maps and books about the area may save a few hundred pounds or stop you from buying the wrong house. Once you have studied the map you will begin to get an idea of what houses are worth visiting. This will save money, time and temper on fruitless visits. Once you know the price at which houses in particular roads tend to be offered you will have a better idea of how much you ought to pay.

What if you are buying at a time of fiercely rising prices? Can you afford the time to do all this patient spadework? Probably not, but unless you have very suddenly come into money you will have gathered experience long before. You don't have to start house-hunting at the age of eleven but try not to be pushed by inexperience and disappointment into buying the first house that is not snapped up under your nose. It may be available because it was turned down for a mortgage, or it may be overpriced.

What newspapers are most worth looking at? Most of the national newspapers carry house advertisements; some devote special days to houses. The Sunday papers also give a certain amount of information: you may well find that the Sunday papers you enjoy reading also carry advertisements for your kind of house.

Most newsagents stock one or several of the papers specializing in house advertisements. The most important and comprehensive are *Dalton's Weekly*, *Exchange and Mart* and the *Property and Business Advertiser*, and for London and the Home Counties the *London Weekly Advertiser*.

There are also the glossy monthly magazines. They deal chiefly with new estates in the course of being built and can be very useful if you are planning ahead: you will probably know the price well in advance and buy a house designed for easy selling and possibly with a ready source of mortgage money. Estate developers frequently arrange with a building society that it will grant mortgages to buyers of sufficiently high income. In times when there are more houses than buyers you sometimes get useful extras thrown in, for example a year's free mortgage or a fitted carpet. Owners of existing houses hope to sell quickly and tend to advertise in the dailies or weeklies. Those looking for beautiful country houses will probably consult *Country Life*; surprisingly, magazines like *The Lady* also contain useful house advertisements.

Once the area of search has been roughly fixed, the local paper of that area is likely to prove the most useful guide to houses. The next step, therefore, is to find out what papers circulate in particular parts of the country. This is where the local library will probably be able to help. It will stock useful publications such as the *Newspaper Press Directory* or *Willing's Press Guide*, from which can be seen not only what papers circulate where, but also where to get them, how much they cost and on what days of the week they appear.

Most advertisements are inserted by estate agents. There is a certain uniformity of language about them which will be explained in the chapter on estate agents. Some advertisements sound more attractive because they were put in either by an imaginative owner, or by an agent who does not belong to one of the professional institutions. Chartered surveyors and members of certain other professional bodies have to keep their advertisements within a fairly narrow framework. Remember: more interestingly worded advertisements do not necessarily describe better houses.

You are looking for two things in the advertisements: what kind of house can you get in that area for the money at your disposal? And who are the estate agents in the district? When you have looked at a few advertisements you can write to some of these agents and ask them for details of possible houses. It will cost no more than a stamp to write for particulars, either to private advertisers or to estate agents. When writing to an agent be careful not to do more than ask for particulars. You do not want unwittingly to engage an agent to find a house for you and to make yourself responsible for his fee.

A letter on the following lines is quite safe:

To a private advertiser

Dear Sir,

I have seen your advertisement of a three-bedroomed house at the price of £   in today's *New Standard*. Could you please let me have particulars.

Yours faithfully,

To an estate agent

Dear Sir,

I am looking for a three-bedroomed house in the Wythenshawe area, if possible built between 1930 and 1939. Price up to £

Could you please let me have particulars of houses which might be suitable. Is the one in   Road advertised in today's *New Standard* still available?

Yours faithfully,

You can, without incurring any liability for estate agents' fees, write similar letters to as many agents as you wish. The result will probably be a flood of printed matter. Most of this you will find useful chiefly as scribbling paper, but gradually you will get an idea of the kind of house you can expect for the price which you are prepared to pay.

If this is a time when prices are going up faster than the daffodils (wild price rises usually happen in spring) and you must join the rush, here are a few hints:

if possible don't buy before you have explored the market;

in times of shortage, keep in close touch with the more active estate agents in your chosen area. They may well not send circulars when houses are snapped up on their doorstep;

when houses are easy to sell many owners sell privately. Tell your friends and colleagues at work that you are looking for a house. They may know someone who wants to sell;

you could even try pushing circular letters through a few letter boxes in your favoured district, but make it clear you are not an estate agent in disguise. You could try something like:

> My wife and I are desperate for a house in or near   as I am starting a new job on . Do you happen to know anyone who wants to sell? We should be so grateful if you would let us know and shall of course refund your expenses. We have been promised a mortgage in principle and could pay up to £

Don't forget your address and telephone number at home and at work. It is a long shot, but it could work.

Before you decide what price you can afford, please read the chapters on what it costs and how to get a mortgage. You cannot form working plans till you know (1) what mortgage you are likely to get, and (2) how much it will cost, first to buy, and then to run, a house. After this you will probably want to make a second list, a sadder and wiser list, distinguishing between essentials and desirables.

When they had looked at various newspapers, Tom and May found they would have to decide whether to try for a rented flat, buy a new house outside town or an older one in the town. They felt that if they were to go on paying rent, they would never be able to afford a house. On the other hand, if they were to buy now, their house ought to be worth more by the time they wanted to sell it again. This would make it possible for them to put a larger deposit on their next house. The choice narrowed down to a house on a new estate outside the old city, which would be easy to resell, and a house in the Victorian part of the town. Their second list was made with the help of the local newspaper and details they had received from a number of estate agents.

Libby had by now decided to look for a terrace house on an estate with lots of children. She rang some of the well-known developers and received details of houses built during the past few years. She eventually decided to concentrate on an area about twenty miles distant from her mother. She deferred a decision on whether to put most of her money into a new house – either buying a bigger one or moving to a more expensive area – or whether to buy a more modest house and put money away for emergencies. Once upon a time saving was a great virtue. At a time of high inflation and low rates of interest, saving in a bank or building society account may be an assured way of losing money. Many people spend as much as they dare on their house.

> *Libby's second list*
> Area – Waverley Road or Glentree Estate
> Town house
> Price – up to £x thousand
> Walking distance first school, playgroup, park.

Peter realized that he had to choose between the comforts of a house well away from London and a humbler living standard in the capital. Although salaries may be higher in London, his extra earnings would not pay for a considerably higher mortgage. He decided on comfort and employment in the country. He applied for jobs and after each hopeful interview bought the local newspapers. The second list was easily made as soon as Peter had a definite job offer.

> *Peter's second list*
> Area – 10 miles from place of work
> Near school – if possible on same side of main road
> Large garden
> Price – approximately three times* Peter's earnings – perhaps slightly more if he got a good price for his present house.

One house was rejected because it was a long way from the village. Peter's wife did not really want to drive a car, and did not trust herself to remember every bit of shopping if she could reach a shop only once a week.

Another house was advertised as being close to the water's edge, overlooking the river. Peter knew that the river was tidal and the chances were that for some six hours each day the house would

---

*This is not a fixed formula. You can easily:

   i) work out approximately how much you will get for your present house;

   ii) deduct your present mortgage and the expenses connected with the sale and the move;

   iii) add your new mortgage, then make your decision.

Peter, in London, would probably need the maximum mortgage he could get on his income. In the country, he could manage on a good deal less.

overlook not water, but mud. An inquiry of the agent confirmed this: although neither estate agent nor owner is under any duty to volunteer information about the demerits of a house, they must give honest answers to questions. If they mislead you, you may have a legal claim against them.

At the same time as looking for a house Peter and his wife also looked for suitable schools for their children and decided to try to find a house within walking distance of a primary school for their two younger children. When the children were old enough to go to a secondary school they would be able to cope with a bus journey.

Your Second List

After a few weeks of looking at newspapers, answering advertisements and corresponding with estate agents you will have enough information to make a visit worth while, even if it means travelling some distance. Prepare for the visit by:

reading at least Part 1 of this book;

reading about the particular type of home which interests you, e.g. flats, new houses, leaseholds. You can easily find the relevant bits from the index on pp. 173–6;

arming yourself with a map or street guide. You may well be able to borrow this from your public library;

telling some of the estate agents that you will be coming, and asking whether they can arrange for you to see houses;

fixing appointments with a few house-owners.

The agent who looks most like having your kind of home may be willing to take you to several houses: a great convenience if you travel by public transport. But leave enough time for going round the district on your own – wander round and get the feel of the neighbourhood. What shops are there? You do not merely want to know where the nearest grocer is, but whether the shops and the shoppers are homely or smart or exotic. Is there a bookshop, betting shop, theatre, tennis club, church, Rotary Club, bingo hall, disco, park, playground – or whatever your family is interested in? Where are the schools (if you have children), doctor or hospital (if you have invalids in the family)?

You may already know the answers if the area is one with which you are familiar. If you are moving to a new area try to find time for just roaming. Walk around pubs, shops and cafés; look for clubs and discotheques. This not only makes for a pleasant afternoon but may stop you from moving to a place where you would feel like outsiders.

The more time you can spend on this part of your search the better. You are more likely to find out whether you would settle happily and how much you should expect to pay for the kind of house you would like.

Here are some hints for different types of buyer:

Moderate Savings, Moderate Income

The choice will probably be between a new house, a converted flat or a small purpose-built flat.

New flats are becoming smaller all the time; if well built and well planned, however, they make a good first purchase. Some builders throw in a number of goodies with which to tempt you, e.g. legal fees, carpets, a TV set. Allow for the fact that these are unlikely to be 'free' and check that the flat itself is worth what you are paying. If you buy carefully, you should make a profit when you sell, particularly in an area where there is a shortage of building land.

A new or newish house on an estate often makes a good family home and is easily resold. It will probably cost more than a flat, old or new, in the same area. Nevertheless, if you have the choice, a house may be better value than a flat. You pay less per square foot, rates tend to be lower comparatively, and the extra space can give you extra scope.

Flats, converted out of Victorian or Edwardian family houses, are very popular with young buyers. You get a lot of space for your money, building societies are prepared to grant as high a mortgage for them as for newer flats, and you can use your energy and ingenuity in making the most of your purchase. But allow for repairs – all old houses need them almost constantly – and also allow for the higher cost of decorating and heating. Your solicitor will be able to tell whether you are responsible under the lease for keeping your own flat in good repair, or for a share of the cost of repairing the entire building. If the latter, do get a surveyor's report on the whole house before you commit yourself to buying: a new roof can cost a lot of money.

A small family will probably find a small modern house the best buy. Such a property tends to keep its price and be easily saleable, and the mortgage payments should not be crippling. A larger family is more comfortable in a bigger house. It may also, with luck, have enough able-bodied members to help pay the mortgage and assist with the repairs an older building inevitably needs and keeps needing.

Low Savings, Rising Income

Take maximum mortgage. Consider borrowing on second mortgage to buy the best house within your grasp. Your rising income should enable you to pay off the expensive second mortgage. But watch out – your low savings may be due to your liking to live up to the limit of your means.

Two or More People Sharing

A married couple is limited to tax relief on a mortgage of £30,000 maximum. Two people not married to one another, on the other hand, can get tax relief up to a total mortgage of £30,000 each. So, two friends can choose to buy one home with one mortgage up to £60,000. If the mortgage is for less than £60,000, they can apportion it between themselves as they wish. It will probably be cheapest for the higher tax payer to borrow the first £30,000. Some building societies will lend up to £30,000 each to more than two people, provided the two biggest earners' incomes justify the mortgage amount.

Divorced People

To save tax it is not usually a good idea for the ex-husband to pay the wife's mortgage. Far better to follow Libby's example – she and her husband had a mortgage on the family home, with tax relief on that mortgage. When they divorced, the husband kept the home, the mortgage and the tax relief. He also paid maintenance to Libby and the children under a court order (more tax relief). Libby bought a house with a mortgage of her own, again with tax relief. Tax can be saved equally when the wife and children remain in the family home, the husband pays maintenance under a court order, the wife takes over the mortgage on the home, and the husband gets a mortgage of his own.

Older People

Usually aim at paying off the mortgage before retirement. Try to take up your last big mortgage by the age of about fifty (if not before). In an assured occupation you can get a fifteen-year mortgage without much difficulty. A person with a good pension could well consider leaving a small mortgage outstanding because of its welcome tax relief: it may make it possible to buy a slightly more luxurious house.

Many people move house when they retire. Consider before you cut yourself off from friends and relatives whether the seaside is the best place for you in the unfriendly days of February. If you plan to retire a long way from your present home, try to get to know the place of your choice and its people before breaking all your links with home. Maybe you work in town and already have a cottage in the country to which you want to retire. You can sell your 'main residence' in town free of capital gains tax and move to the country.

Sheltered Housing for the Elderly

Small bungalows and flats are now being specially built for the elderly. There is usually provision for a resident warden who can be called in an emergency. The lay-out of each bungalow or flat should make it easy for elderly people to move around. Well planned accommodation should provide for easy access to the door, for moving about in a wheelchair if necessary, for electric plugs to be at table height, and for an alarm system allowing people to contact the warden.

Advantages:	You own your home
	Your home is saleable
	The warden can help if you are disabled or become ill
Snags:	A 24-hour warden service is expensive
	The more comprehensive the service, the more it will cost
Check carefully:	Does the service charge include hot water, central heating, upkeep of the garden, maintenance of the outside of the building, repainting the inside?
	How many wardens are there? One warden cannot be on duty 24 hours a day, 7 days a week.
	Is there an easy-to-use alarm system in every room, including kitchen and W C?
	How far from shops, buses, doctor, hospital etc. is the house?
	Is there double glazing, roof insulation? If the house is draughty, heating costs will be higher.

Moving in a Hurry

If you are faced with a sudden move and no time to explore, it is probably wisest to choose a newish standard house, e.g. in a terrace built during the last fifteen years, or a semi-detached house up to forty years old. It is relatively easy to find out the current price for such properties and to sell them again when you have found one nearer your ideal. Also, you should get a mortgage without too much trouble. Buying from an owner who has already found a house to move to may be quicker than buying from someone who has only recently decided to move and who may change his mind or fail to get a mortgage.

Important: For All Would-Be House-buyers

Many tax savings can be made by house-buyers. Remember: it is cheaper to borrow on a mortgage than to take out a bank overdraft or juggle your credit cards. There is tax relief on a mortgage but not on a bank loan; it is therefore cheaper to get a higher mortgage to buy or improve your house and pay cash for a car or a holiday.

Chapter 3

Where Will the Money Come From?

Money for house-buying can be borrowed from local authorities, building societies, insurance companies, banks, trust funds or rich relations. For the majority of us, it comes from building societies – set up for the express purpose of lending out money, in the form of mortgages, which other members of the public (the depositors) have lent to them. The system has stood the test of time rather better than those operated by banks, who move in and out of the mortgage market somewhat unpredictably. When you start thinking about house-buying you would probably be wiser to save with a building society than with a bank, particularly as many building societies now provide cheque books or cash dispensers to make it easy for you to pay your bills out of your building society account. In the meantime, the money in the building society earns interest as well as staking your claim for a mortgage. You can also ask them to give you a rough idea of how much you can expect to borrow.

Unfortunately I know of no recipe which will guarantee the exact loan you want at the moment you want it. This is another reason why it is often a good idea to put your savings for the house into one, or possibly several, building societies. Many societies, when they are short of money for lending, give mortgages only to people who already have money deposited with them. It helps if you can be one of the favoured few. At the same time, do not expect the building society to turn away the multitudes in your favour simply because you have had a few hundred pounds invested for the past two weeks. Visit one or two societies as soon as you make up your mind to buy a house (or even earlier). If you are well received, put your savings in. Call back from time to time to check whether lending conditions have changed. If you are treated to a long face and news of a long waiting list, try the building society next door: if you get a better reception there, transfer your money. It is your only weapon.

Waiting List

The money which a building society lends out normally comes from funds which others have deposited with that society. People are keener on putting their savings into a building society when it pays more interest than a bank than when it pays less. This balance changes frequently. When a building society is short of money to lend, it uses one of several controls: it may give new loans only to people who already have a mortgage with the society (i.e. those who sell one house and buy another), or to people who have savings invested in it, or to first-time buyers. The needs of even these selected groups sometimes exceed the money available. The building society then rations its loans. You may be told: 'Yes, you can have the money you have asked for', but 'No, you cannot have it before February'. When waiting lists are the order of the day, sellers are usually prepared to wait. When mortgages are easy to come by, there is no need for waiting lists.

How to Get a Mortgage

Whether the money comes from a building society or not, house loans have much in common:

(1) You will get a loan only if the lender approves of your house, of yourself and of your income.

(2) You have to pay interest on the mortgage and will probably get tax relief.

(3) The type of mortgage most warmly recommended is not necessarily the one that is best for you.

(4) You will have to sign (and obey the terms of) a mortgage document.

(5) You will not get the deeds of the house while you owe any money under the mortgage.

The House

Every building society likes best to lend on a house built traditionally of bricks or stone and with a tiled roof, either detached, semi-detached or terraced. A modern purpose-built leasehold flat will be equally popular. A house should be either freehold or on a very long lease. 'Freehold' means that both the house and the ground on which it stands belong to their owner for ever. 'Leasehold' means that the ground underneath the house belongs to *A* who lets the house itself on a long lease (often 99 or 999 years) to *B*. At the end of the lease the ownership of the house goes back to *A*, or – more likely – to his great-grandson, or to the person who has in the meantime bought the freehold reversion from *A*. If there are only a few years of a lease left, no building society is likely to lend *B* money on it. A first-time buyer should therefore keep clear of the end of a long lease till he has taken advice from a solicitor. The house could be a bargain if the Leasehold Reform Act allows the occupier to buy the freehold (more about this in Chapter 7). If it does not, or if the freehold costs too much, don't buy that house. Anyone with small savings and the need for the largest possible mortgage loan should look for a newish house, flat or maisonette.

If you have set your heart on an older house or flat, you may be able to get a high mortgage, but you will also have to allow for the higher costs of repairing and maintaining your home. Frequently a building society says that certain repairs must be done before it will hand over the loan money. In recent years many old family houses have been divided into separate flats. A long lease (usually at least 99 years) is then granted for each separate 'converted' flat and each flat can be sold and resold independent of the other flats in the house. Often, instead of making the owner of the top floor flat responsible for the entire roof, the cost of all major repairs is shared by all the flats in the building. Converted flats are popular with young couples – they are larger and cost less than modern homes.

Mortgages can usually also be had for purpose-built flats and for maisonettes. A 'flat' usually shares its door to the street and its stairs with other flats; a 'maisonette' does not.

The House-Buyer

Most building societies are far more interested in the purchasers' income than in the purchasers themselves. Their age matters to some extent: building societies like the mortgage to be repaid before retirement. People in their fifties may therefore have greater difficulty in borrowing money on mortgage than people in their twenties, and will have to accept a mortgage for a shorter term. However, if you have had a mortgage for many years and have always punctually paid your monthly instalments, you will probably have no difficulty in getting another mortgage from the same society, whatever your age. Equally, if you can look forward to an assured pension, the building society will probably welcome you as a borrower.

The applicant's sex matters less than it used to: a woman with an assured income, such as a teacher or a nurse, will have very little difficulty in borrowing. Complaints often come from girls in freelance occupations who resent being patronized by building society managers. However, their male counterparts find it equally hard to get a loan before their business is visibly well established. Building societies are keen on seeing audited accounts for at least two consecutive years, showing a healthy profit.

Your Income

This is of far greater interest to the building society than personal circumstances, but here again different societies use different yardsticks. Some societies look at gross income – the amount you earn on paper, disregarding tax etc. – others at net income – the amount you actually take home each week or month. Some societies take overtime into account, some consider all the earnings of both husband and wife, others only a small part of the second income. Some are willing to take into account the income you will get from letting part of the house, others will refuse to lend on a house which is not entirely occupied by you and your family. Having decided on what they consider to be your 'income', different societies use varying formulae for calculating the maximum amount they are prepared to lend. Most societies, whatever complicated formula they use – usually between two-and-a-half and three times your annual gross income – aim at your monthly payments not being more than your weekly net earnings. 'Weekly earnings' can include those of husband and wife, but the total loan is unlikely to be more than just over twice the main income plus between one third and three quarters of the second income. The income of a young wife rates less highly than that of a woman whose family is complete. 'Monthly payments' may mean 'mortgage payments' or 'mortgage plus one twelfth of the annual rates'. Some societies are more interested in how much rent you have been paying in the past, and whether you have paid that rent regularly. If your rent book shows that you managed to pay a high rent on the dot, they are more likely to trust you with a high mortgage.

Tax Relief

MIRAS

If up to now you have been paying rent, you might just possibly be in for a pleasant surprise. MIRAS, 'Mortgage Interest Relief At Source', means that, provided you qualify, you pay mortgage interest less tax at the basic rate. Tax is automatically deducted, so that if your mortgage document says that your interest rate is 11 per cent, you in fact pay only 7·67 per cent. This is one of the few occasions in life when a loan is cheaper than the complicated documents make out. Nor is this all: tax relief is allowed at your highest rate of income tax. Thus, if you pay income tax at 50 per cent on part of your earnings, you can set off the mortgage interest against that part. However, deduction at higher rates is not usually automatic. So tell your Inspector of Taxes as soon as you have bought your house and ask for a higher PAYE code number.

Who Gets Tax Relief

You can claim tax relief on a mortgage up to £30,000 on your home, on the home of your spouse from whom you are separated or on the home of an elderly dependent relative. The tax relief can be split among these if you wish, i.e. you may take out a mortgage on your own house and also one on a house for your mother, so long as the total is not more than £30,000.

Husband and wife are limited to tax relief on a maximum of £30,000 even if both have dependent relatives.

Single people, on the other hand, even if they are living together, can have separate mortgage tax relief and can split the mortgage payments to their best advantage. Taking a £40,000 mortgage as an example, the person with the higher tax rate can be responsible for a mortgage up to the limit of £30,000, and the one in a lower bracket for the remaining £10,000. But they must watch out: if they decide to get married, the second tax relief will vanish. The tax man does not seem to approve of the married state. (See also p. 30.)

Divorced and separated couples can each have tax relief. A separated or divorced woman should, if possible, get her own mortgage (plus, if need be, maintenance from her ex-husband) rather than live in a house owned by him. (More of this on p. 31.)

	Method of Tax Relief	*Do You Have to Make a Claim*
Mortgage of £30,000 or under		
Basic rate taxpayer	MIRAS	No
Higher rate taxpayer	Part MIRAS/part claim	Higher rate: yes
Mortgage over £30,000		
Basic rate taxpayer	Relief only up to £30,000	Yes*
Higher rate taxpayer	Relief only up to £30,000	Yes*

*Some building societies use MIRAS.

The Best Mortgage For You

Assuming you are buying at a time when mortgages are easy to come by, or are buying a reasonably popular type of house, or do not need to borrow a very high percentage of the house price, you may be able to choose what kind of mortgage is best for you rather than grab what is offered. For most people a Repayment Mortgage with a mortgage protection policy or a Low Cost Endowment Mortgage are the best buys. But do not take my word for this. Decide what you need. A young couple may want the highest possible loan, the lowest possible repayments for the first few years, and enough insurance to pay off the mortgage if one party should die. An elderly person without dependants, on the other hand, may want a small mortgage and no insurance on it. Once you have decided on your needs, find out what is available. The pros and cons of different types of mortgages are set out in this chapter.

Try not to be dazzled by the thrilling offers which are bound to come your way. They may be intended to get publicity rather than benefit you. Make sure you get a detailed written proposal of what it is you are being offered, take it home and look at it quietly. Never sign anything on your first visit. Also, have a look at least at the first part of Chapter 4, 'The Cost of Buying and Running a House'.

Building Society Repayment Mortgage

As a building society repayment mortgage forms a good yardstick against which to measure the advantages and disadvantages of other mortgages, let us look more closely at some typical clauses in a repayment mortgage document:

Calculation of Interest

1. The society shall be entitled in any year to charge interest on the amount of the total debt on the last day of the immediately preceding year and to enter interest for the year in the account of the borrower on the first or any subsequent day in the year.

Though you repay a little of the loan with each monthly payment, the building society is likely to calculate interest on what you owe at the beginning of each year and collect that amount of interest each month. Let us say you pay with each instalment of interest a further £50 of capital. In a year you will therefore repay £600. At the beginning of the year interest on your mortgage is calculated to include that £600; by December you will have paid back all but £50 of it but your repayments won't go down until January. At the end of the year you are paying at a higher gross rate of interest than stated in the mortgage. An interest rate of 11·25 per cent gross, calculated once a year, is equivalent to a 'true' interest rate of nearly 12 per cent before tax relief. Ask the building society to tell you the true interest rate (official term APR, 'Annual Percentage Rate') if you wish to compare various offers.

Change in the Interest Rate

2. The society may from time to time vary the interest rate. For an increase in the interest rate the society must give the borrower at least seven days' notice in writing.

All building societies and most other lenders reserve the right to change the rate of interest from time to time. When the rate of interest goes up, either the monthly mortgage payments go up correspondingly or the period of the mortgage is extended. Sometimes the building society decides; sometimes the borrower is asked whether he would rather pay more each month or go on paying longer.

Monthly Payments

3. The borrower will discharge the primary obligations of the borrower by making to the society on the payment day in every month a combined payment (which will be the same amount as the monthly payment) comprising
    a) the relevant loan interest after deducting thereout a sum equal to income tax thereon at the basic rate and
    b) a component of capital.

The monthly payment under the mortgage is more than one twelfth of the annual interest laid down by the terms of the mortgage because you gradually repay the mortgage itself. Hence the name 'repayment mortgage'. With mortgages granted before 1983 the borrower paid more interest (and received more tax relief) in the first ten or fifteen years than he did in the last five or ten years of his mortgage. Since the introduction of MIRAS (see p. 38), many lenders calculate monthly payments in such a way that you get the same tax relief throughout the term of the mortgage. This means that the buyer who sells his house every few years pays rather more for his mortgage than he did under the old system. A few building societies and most banks are prepared to calculate interest as in the pre-MIRAS days – it is worth asking about this if you are getting a mortgage at a time when lenders are keen to do business and you do not expect to remain in your house for at least ten years.

These are some of the more important clauses; in one form or another they occur in every repayment mortgage, but they are not highlighted and often disappear in the middle of many other clauses. Often, particularly in 'simple' modern mortgage forms, you are referred to the society's rules for details. Do not accept that the simpler form means a simpler life, or a mortgage more benefi-cial to you. This warning goes for all sorts of mortgage!

To sum up the pros and cons of a repayment mortgage:

Advantages:	Repayment spread over many years
	Income tax relief
	Offered by all building societies
Snag:	You need to allow for a mortgage protec-tion policy if your death during the currency of the mortgage would mean financial problems for your family
Worth investigating:	by every would-be borrower, if only as a means of comparing with other methods.

Here is a selection of other types of mortgage:

Mortgage Plus Guarantee Policy

When you ask a building society for a mortgage, it will instruct a surveyor to inspect the house and to recommend how much the society may safely lend on it. (House-buyers often think of this inspection as a 'survey', though building societies are anxious to point out that it is nothing of the kind.) Building societies do not usually lend more than about 80 per cent of the value put on the house by their surveyor. In fact, however, there are many loans of 90 per cent and 95 per cent; even loans of 100 per cent are sometimes available. The top slice of the loan is guaranteed by an insurance policy for which you pay one single premium instead of the more usual annual premium. This once-only premium will probably be 3–3½ per cent of the sum guaranteed. The building society will either deduct the premium from the mortgage hand-out, or, if you are lucky, will lend it to you, add it to the mortgage, and recover it gradually and comparatively painlessly over the run of the mortgage. To take an example: I want to buy a house, built in 1955, price £8,000 and ask for a mortgage of £7,500. The building society offers £6,400, plus an additional £1,100 backed by a guarantee policy. The policy costs £41·25 which is added to the mortgage.

The total mortgage, therefore, is   £6,400

plus   1,100

plus   41·25
_____

£7,541·25
_____

Advantages: As for repayment mortgage

Can bring mortgage advance up beyond 80 per cent

Snags: As for repayment mortgage

Insurance premium may increase your capital contribution (if payable in one sum) or your mortgage instalments (if added to the mortgage)

You may have to pay a higher rate of interest for a higher than usual loan.

Index Linking

A way of starting with comparatively low monthly payments.

As with an ordinary repayment mortgage, your monthly payments consist of a combination of interest and capital. The rate of interest charged by the lender is lower than usual, and the loan can be as high as $3\frac{1}{2}$ times your income. The snag is that the capital you owe (the mortgage amount) is *not* fixed but goes up in line with inflation. When you come to sell, therefore, your mortgage is likely to be much higher than when you bought.

    Advantage: Low monthly payments at beginning
        Snag: Uncertainty about how much you will have to pay back when you sell the house
               Could be risky.

Endowment Mortgage

You apply to a building society or bank as in the case of a repayment mortgage. You do not repay the loan by instalments but leave it outstanding throughout. You also take out an endowment insurance (a type of life policy) for the same amount and period and assign this policy to the lender. When the policy matures it is used to pay back the mortgage. If you die during the mortgage term, the insurance policy matures immediately, repays your mortgage, and no further premiums or mortgage interest fall due.

As with a repayment mortgage you make regular monthly or quarterly payments. But under this scheme your payments consist of (1) interest on the mortgage and (2) premiums on the endowment insurance.

Be warned: the reason for recommending an endowment mortgage may be that the lender is more interested in the commission his organization will receive on endowment policies than in what is best for you. Check the figures carefully – some policies benefit you more than others. Ask whether the mortgage interest will be the same as for a repayment mortgage or whether it will be higher. It may well cost $\frac{1}{4} - \frac{1}{2}$ per cent more.

With Profits Endowment

You take out a policy for the full amount of the mortgage. The policy shares in the profits of the insurance company, declared every so often. At the end of the mortgage period you should therefore get a capital sum (representing your share of the profits) in addition to having your mortgage repaid. Lovely – but remember that this bonanza won't reach you for another twenty or twenty-five years, even if you sell your house and repay your mortgage in a few years from now. In twenty years, what now looks like a fantastic lot of money may not be worth so very much.

Without Profits Endowment

This is similar to the other endowment policy, except that the monthly insurance premium is lower and there is no bonanza at the end of the mortgage term. The mortgage is repaid when the policy matures, and that's it.

Not usually a good idea.

Low Cost Endowment

Instead of a £20,000 insurance policy to protect a £20,000 mortgage, the insurance company will offer an endowment policy with profits for, say, £10,000, coupled with a 'term insurance' for the balance of the mortgage loan. That combined premium is cheaper than for an ordinary endowment policy with profits; the term insurance makes sure that the mortgage is repaid should you die during the mortgage term. With any luck the 'with profits' policy will be worth more than the mortgage amount by the time you have to redeem your mortgage.

This scheme was very popular before the 1984 budget took away tax relief on insurance premiums. Since then, however, more and more schemes have been based on optimism rather than sound financial planning. With many low cost schemes there is no guaranteed sum at the end of the mortgage period. The monthly payments may be lower than for a repayment mortgage, but you may not get enough at the end of the mortgage period to pay off your mortgage.

Before deciding on an endowment policy, of whatever type, it is important to get quotations from several insurance companies. You could do this through an insurance broker or by answering a few newspaper advertisements. The conditions offered by different companies can vary considerably. Make sure you compare like with like by asking each company for a detailed quotation based on the same assumptions, e.g. a mortgage for twenty-five years for £x thousand at y per cent for a man aged thirty, secured by a with profits endowment policy. You could ask for two different quotations, the second for a low start policy or for a policy on the joint lives of husband and wife. The difference in price between 'single life' and 'joint lives' of husband and wife is often quite small. A joint lives policy means that the policy money is paid out on the death of either the husband or the wife before it matures.

When you have found out which companies offer a good bargain, check how easy it would be to transfer the policy to another house should you want to move during its currency – as you almost certainly will. Taking an endowment mortgage does not mean that you are stuck with the same house for the next twenty-five years. When you sell your house, you have three options:

(1) You can keep your policy going. If you are taking out a bigger mortgage on the new house, you can take out a further insurance policy for the excess. Alternatively, it may be cheaper to divide your mortgage: endowment for the original amount, repayment for the balance.

(2) You can make your insurance policy a 'paid up policy'. This means that you pay no further premiums but leave your past payments with the insurance company till the policy matures. You will obviously get less at the end of the twenty-five years than if you continue paying.

(3) You surrender the policy for a cash sum. Be sure to get comparative figures from the insurance company before you decide. Surrender values can be disappointingly low.

You are unlikely to find an ordinary endowment policy a particularly good bargain, though you may be forced or cajoled into getting an endowment policy as a condition of being granted a mortgage at all.

Try in the first place to get a mortgage direct from a building society rather than through a broker. If the building society offers you an endowment mortgage, ask whether it would still give you a mortgage if you decided on repayment rather than endowment. Should the building society insist on endowment, you will have to grin and bear it or start your search again. Many building societies leave the choice to you. In that case, you may well find a repayment mortgage, backed by a mortgage protection policy, or possibly a low cost endowment policy, the best bargain. But endowment mortgages do have advantages for some people:

Advantages: Policy can act as health insurance: it cannot be cancelled whatever your state of health might be in the future

Tax relief is greater than under repayment scheme

Low life insurance premiums for young borrowers

Life insurance continues even if you sell the house

Snags: Payments continue even if your fortunes fall and you no longer pay high income tax

Insurance premiums continue even if you sell the house

Surrender value of policy may be small

Mortgage interest may be higher than for repayment mortgage

If mortgage interest rate goes up, your monthly payments will have to go up – the mortgage term is not easily extended

The profits element in a 'with profits' policy is based on hope; there is no guarantee of profits.

Worth investigating: by anyone who pays high tax and expects to continue that way

    by anyone who values a life insurance policy
      regardless of house-ownership

    by anyone who cannot otherwise get the
      mortgage he wants.

Higher Loans

Few building societies now put a fixed upper limit on how much
they are prepared to lend on any one house. The maximum will
depend on income and on the value of the house. However, many
building societies charge a higher rate of interest on loans above
a certain figure – £15,000 for some societies, more for others.
Banks and insurance companies on the other hand are often quite
keen on high loans for expensive houses. For a loan of over
£15,000, therefore, get quotations from a building society, a bank
and an insurance company. Be sure to ask for exactly the same
mortgage from each. If you don't, you will not be able to compare
like with like. And do not forget to ask a bank or insurance
company whether they will charge any kind of fee other than for
inspecting the house. Most banks do; building societies don't.

    A 'higher' loan from an insurance company direct, at fixed rates
of interest, could be an advantage if you are borrowing at a time
when interest rates are low but are expected to go up. It is advisable
to shop around, not only to compare rates but also to see what
insurance cover is offered or insisted upon.

Unit Linked Mortgage

You pay insurance premiums as for an endowment mortgage.
Each premium is invested in unit trusts; there is no guaranteed
capital sum when your policy matures. You are really playing the
stock market through the medium of your insurance company,
who may very well be expert investors. If they are successful, you
may do better than with a conventional 'with profits' policy. But
if your units do badly, you may not be able to repay your mortgage.
Insurance companies therefore sometimes combine this scheme
with a policy ensuring – for a monthly premium – that there will

not be a deficit. Tempting for anyone who fancies the stock market without having spare money to invest.

Snags: Risky, possibly expensive

Not accepted by many building societies.

Pension Mortgage

This is available only to people who are self-employed or to those who have no occupational pension scheme. These two groups, in order to encourage them to save for their old age, get tax relief on annual payments they choose to make for their retirement. Instead of taking out a separate endowment policy (on which there is no tax relief) the house-buyer takes out a pension policy, or uses an existing pension scheme.

Advantage: Very tax effective

Snags: Tax relief limited to a percentage of your income

Pension money becomes available only when you retire

Not accepted by every lender

Eats into your retirement pension.

Loan Above £30,000

There is no legal restriction on how much can be borrowed to buy a house. Negotiations are between you and the lender. Tax legislation does, however, say that there is tax relief only on approved mortgages up to £30,000. There is no tax relief on the excess.

Top Up Loan

Not a mortgage to choose, but one you may have to put up with if the building society won't lend you what you need. It is possible that an insurance company will agree to lend the balance on a second mortgage at a higher rate of interest and subject to an endowment policy, probably on the whole amount of the two mortgages. Such a loan can be very expensive at the time it is made but is popular in times of high inflation. The first years may be tough, but as payments are pegged while the value of your house and your income go up, this kind of arrangement has many followers among rising young executives. Such a scheme needs not only a good income, but also respectable savings. The entire loan is unlikely to exceed 75 per cent of the value of the house.

Advantages: High mortgage possible
              May help you buy more expensive house
              Tax relief
Snags: High cost of buying – legal fees for house and for
                  two mortgages
              High monthly payments – two mortgages plus
                  insurance premium
              Tax relief only up to £30,000 mortgage
              High interest rate on second mortgage
              Not every building society uses this scheme.

Local Authority Mortgage

Local authorities usually lend only on houses in their area. They often lend on houses less favoured by building societies (for example, houses built before the First World War; houses built on more than two floors), but their mortgage funds are limited, and at times when money is short local authorities frequently have to stop lending. Many local authorities lend only to tenants buying their council houses and to people who have been refused a building society mortgage.

A point for those with gambling instinct: the local authority may well lend at a fixed rate of interest, i.e. the interest will not go up or down like a building society mortgage. If you get your mortgage at a time when interest rates are low, you may save a lot over the years. I know a man who felt he could never move from his house as he had borrowed at what sixteen years later seemed like a ridiculously low rate of interest. The problem is to be right in judging whether the interest rate is high or low.

Advantages: May lend on 'difficult' houses

May give 100 per cent mortgage

Not every authority investigates borrower's income

May give a longer term loan, which means lower monthly repayments

Snags: Rate of interest often higher than that of building society

Some authorities lend only to council tenants

Authorities frequently run out of money for loans.

Worth investigating: by all would-be borrowers at times when interest rates are low

by anyone who cannot get a building society mortgage

Home Loan

A home loan is unlikely to solve your mortgage problem but is a pleasant extra offered by the state to first-time buyers. This is what you have to do to qualify:

(1) Open a home loan account with a building society or savings bank. You have to fill in a special form: make sure to ask for this – you cannot join the scheme until you have filled in the right piece of paper.

(2) Save into that account for two years.

(3) Make sure that at the end of Year One you have at least £300 in the account.

(4) Keep at least £300 in the account for the whole of Year Two.

(5) Better still, bring your account up to £600 before applying for a mortgage.

(6) £600, when you apply for the mortgage, qualifies you for an extra mortgage loan of £600, interest free for up to five years. £300 or more in the account for all of the year before you apply for a mortgage qualifies for a tax-free bonus of between £40 (for a £300 deposit) and £110 (for £1,000 or more).

(7) The best sum to keep in the account would seem to be £300 in the first year and £1,000 in the second. This will give tax-free interest of £110 plus an extra loan of £600 which can be added to your mortgage.

(8) The scheme can be used only for houses below price limits laid down by the government. The limits in 1984 ranged from £19,200 in Humberside to £33,100 in Greater London and are changed from time to time.

Guaranteed Loan

A bank or building society from time to time tries to encourage depositors by promising a mortgage to regular savers. A mortgage may be guaranteed to anyone who regularly deposits money for at least eighteen months. Interest on these deposit accounts is usually somewhat lower than on ordinary savings accounts. The amount guaranteed depends on how much has been deposited, and usually is x many times (at present anything from four to ten times) the total deposited. Thus, if you save £100 per month for eighteen months you might get a guaranteed mortgage of as little as £7,200 or as much as £18,000. The lender will still want to be satisfied that the house is suitable and that your income is high enough to allow you to make the monthly mortgage payments. The advantage of the scheme is that you might get a mortgage at a time of mortgage famine when others don't.

I would suggest putting money into the Home Loan scheme first, unless you are on the point of getting married. Barclays Bank have quite an attractive 'Getting Married' scheme.

Advantages:	Makes sure of a mortgage
	You can change your mind and withdraw your money
Snags:	Guaranteed mortgage schemes are not always available
	You must save regularly
	Lower than average interest on savings.

100 Per Cent Mortgages

These are rare except for sitting tenants of private landlords and for tenants of local authorities. Both groups can often buy their houses at less than market value and building societies are usually happy to lend the whole purchase price. Local authorities, when offering a house to a tenant, offer a mortgage at the same time. Sometimes building society lending rates are more favourable than those of local authorities. It is worth checking before buying your council house.

Occasionally there are other opportunities for 100 per cent mortgages but you may well find that the lender values the house at less than the price you are asked to pay. 100 per cent means: 100 per cent of the value put on the house by the lender. The buyer has to find the difference, as well as the usual fees.

Low Start Mortgage

Instead of paying the same amount year after year, you pay less in the early years of the mortgage and more later. The maximum rate of payment is usually reached at the end of either five or ten years. Some insurance companies combine the low cost endowment scheme with a 'low start' scheme, where insurance premiums start low but go up every year. They may continue to rise throughout the currency of the policy. A low start scheme can sometimes be combined with a pension mortgage (p. 49).

Advantages:	Costs less than other mortgages at the start
	May bring a house within your reach when you are only beginning to earn
	You may be able to get a higher loan than with other mortgage schemes
	Higher mortgage payments in the future may be affordable because your income has gone up
Snags:	The cost of the mortgage may go up faster than your income
	Payments may be high when your children are

at their most expensive and when your wife is
not earning

Interest on this sort of mortgage may be higher
than usual.

Private Loan

Mortgages can sometimes be arranged out of trust funds either
within the family or through a solicitor. Unlike other mortgages,
private mortgages are often given for an indefinite period. When
the lender wants his money back, he gives the borrower notice; the
length of notice is fixed in the mortgage – usually at around six
months. In the meantime the borrower pays interest on the loan.
The lender often insists on a life insurance policy on the borrower's
life, as additional security for the loan.

Advantage: Can sometimes be had for a lower rate of interest
             within the family, or from an employer

Snags: Not easy to come by

         Interest rates may be high

         Lender may demand repayment at a time when
         you do not have and cannot raise the money
         to repay.

Loan by Employer

Some large firms (for example, banks) offer mortgages at low rates
of interest to members of their staff. From the employee's point of
view an even better scheme is one whereby the employer helps
with the monthly mortgage payments. The subsidy is taxable in
the employee's hands but his tax relief on the mortgage is not
reduced by the subsidy. Such loans will either have to be repaid
when the employee leaves the firm or the monthly payments will
then go up to a commercial level.

Advantage: Lower monthly mortgage payments may enable
             you to buy a house you could not otherwise
             afford

Snag: Even if mortgage is cheaper than average, rates
and other outgoings are not
You may find it difficult to change jobs.

Unless you stay with the same firm till the mortgage is paid off,
it is safer to buy a house within your means at normal rates of
mortgage interest.

Mortgage Brokers and Insurance Brokers

Brokers do not lend money but may be able to find a mortgage for
you. Insurance brokers are unlikely to charge for finding a
mortgage but will expect you to take out an insurance policy (see
Endowment Mortgage and the warning on p. 44). Mortgage
brokers charge a fee for their service: find out at the start how
much. You may still have to take out an insurance policy.

Advantage: You might get enough money to buy a house
when conventional sources have failed
Snags: Neither service is cheap nor will it lead to low
monthly outgoings – check carefully whether
you can afford them
The fact that a building society has considered it
risky to lend to you might just possibly be based
on sound argument.

Remember
No one type of mortgage is a 'best buy' for everyone *but*:

some building societies charge a higher rate of interest for
mortgages above a certain figure. This higher rate, and when it
should start, is independently decided by each society – there is no
rule about it. If you are offered a mortgage at a higher rate, consider
shopping around;

an endowment mortgage may well mean a higher rate of
interest than a repayment mortgage;

few mortgages run their full course. Most people move house
every seven to ten years, repaying one mortgage and possibly
obtaining another one. Bear this in mind when you work out

whether you should take a repayment mortgage or some form of endowment;

if you have dependants you need an insurance policy to repay the mortgage should you die before the mortgage is paid off. A mortgage protection policy is likely to serve you better than an endowment;

a pension mortgage is tax effective, but eats into your pension.

How Can You Save Money?

One way of ensuring you can afford the house you want is not to spend money where you don't need to spend:

Estate agents fees: As a buyer you should *never* have to pay these. You may possibly get a house at a slightly lower price by buying direct or through one of the property centres.

Survey: Many people do without a survey, but they are taking a risk. You may be able to cut down on the cost by employing the building society surveyor, or by getting a limited report – see Chapter 9, 'Surveyors'.

Solicitors: Even if you feel you can manage without a solicitor, the building society will employ one to make sure its interests are protected. Check with your own solicitor that he will be instructed by the building society you have in mind, or let him suggest a likely building society.

Removal: Unless you have a large quantity of valuable belongings, you may find a move with a rented van a great money saver – see Chapter 14, 'Preparing Your Move'.

Chapter 4

The Cost of Buying and Running a House

'House for Sale. Immaculate condition. £   . 90 per cent mortgage available.'

This kind of advertisement is meant to warm your heart. It might signal the house you can afford though your savings are slender. For a deposit of a mere ten per cent you will be able to buy a house which will almost certainly increase its value quickly. What is more you can take twenty or twenty-five years to pay for it.

Before you rush out, however, read to the end of the chapter and do your sums. Remember the '90 per cent mortgage available' means available only to someone whose income, in the eyes of a building society, is high enough to justify such a large loan. This was explained in Chapter 3, 'Where Will the Money Come From?'

There will also be other expenses, such as stamp duties, land registry fees, legal fees, surveys, building society fees and more besides. In addition, there is the cost of running the home: the more you borrow on mortgage, the higher this will be.

Do not let this chapter depress you. It is full of figures which, however you look at them, show that it costs a great deal of money to buy a house and that, when you have bought it, it will be expensive to run. For most of us there is little choice; it is practically impossible to find a house to rent – the Rent Acts have seen to this. Not everyone qualifies for council housing. Few people in the long run are happy in a tent, caravan or houseboat – therefore sooner or later they buy a house. Even though the average first-time house-owner may well spend a quarter of his income on mortgage payments alone, the strain gets less as his income rises. By and large, a house usually proves a good investment. Its great charm is that inflation helps the person with the mortgage. Interest rates may go up by one or two per cent every now and then; incomes tend to go up by more. And there is tax relief on the interest payment. A mortgage up to £30,000 on the house in which you live gets tax relief at your highest personal tax rate. What is more, the mortgage itself (the money you borrowed) will not go up at all.

You are unlikely to have the courage to buy a house knowing that tomorrow you will become redundant, *but* your savings are probably better invested in a house than in a bank. For one thing, if you have to put up with prolonged unemployment you will not become eligible for social security benefits while the bulk of your capital is intact. If it is invested in a house, on the other hand, the DHSS will eventually come in on your mortgage payments. Also, your chances of earning money are increased if you have a house: you might take in lodgers or start a new business from your home.

The value of your house will probably keep step with inflation. Even if you have to sell at a time when prices are steady, you will probably find that the house you are buying has not gone up either. This book is not intended for budding financiers but for people who need a home: however expensive and complicated it looks, a home is likely to be the best buy you will make in a lifetime.

The first part of this chapter goes into the cost of buying a house and ends with an estimate. When you have filled in this estimate you will be able to calculate how much of your money to put into the house and how much to borrow on mortgage.

Go and see a building society to get some idea of whether they will lend you that sum. You will not at this stage get a definite promise, nor even a definite figure, but you will get a rough idea and you will also find out what proof they will need of your income. There is much more about mortgages in Chapter 3, 'Where Will the Money Come From?'

The second part of the chapter gives you an idea of what it will cost to run the house. Obviously, you can spend more; I am talking only of the essential running cost. This part is unlikely to be of direct interest to your employer, but it will give you an idea of the kind of income you need to keep up the home you have in mind.

Even if you are fortunate and can get a cheap mortgage through your employers it is worth doing your sums carefully. Paul and his wife Anthea both worked for a bank which offered cheap mortgages to staff. They bought a most glamorous house, relying on a low interest rate. All was fine until after five years they were the proud parents of two small children, Anthea was earning nothing and Paul found he could not cope with mortgage, outgoings on his expensive house, hire purchase payments on his car and the needs of his young family. He required a very much better-paid job but no such job was on hand. He concluded, rather late in the day, that he would have done better to stick to a house within his means and to buy the car out of the money he had saved on mortgage interest.

The Cost of Buying

Capital Contribution

You probably won't be able to borrow all the money it takes to buy a house. Most building societies insist on your putting in some of your own. For your first house this 'capital contribution' – the difference between the price and the mortgage – may well take up all your savings. Once you have a house to sell when you buy another, it tends to get easier.

Solicitors or estate agents can advise you on different types of mortgage and where best to apply. Suppose Tom Jones decides to buy a house for £28,000. He can either put all his savings towards buying the house (and therefore have a smaller mortgage) or he can try to get the highest possible mortgage and keep some of his savings.

As Tom is expecting a rise in salary, he will probably decide to try to get a high mortgage. He can afford the monthly mortgage payments without too much financial strain, he will have to pay enough income tax to make good use of the tax relief on the mortgage interest, and he will have some money left to buy furniture.

It is as well to know when this money has to be paid. The usual practice is for ten per cent of the house price to be paid by the time you exchange contracts (more about contracts on p. 139) and the balance on completion of the sale.

Tom's capital contribution will look like this:

Price of house	£28,000	Pay 10 per cent on exchange of contracts	£2,800
less mortgage	£25,000	plus balance on completion	£200
	£3,000		£3,000

Your capital contribution

Price of house	£	Pay 10 per cent = £	on exchange of contracts
less mortgage	£	balance = £	on completion
	£	Capital contribution	£

Some points to bear in mind:

when you are selling one house to buy another, ten per cent of the price may have to be paid before you have access to any of the money from your old home. If this causes a problem, tell your solicitor as early as possible;

if you are tenants of the house you are buying you may get a 95 or 100 per cent mortgage. Ask how much deposit you need. Local authorities sometimes ask for a token payment on exchange of contracts, even if they offer a 100 per cent mortgage;

the capital contribution is probably your largest single payment; nevertheless, do not forget to allow for all the other payments to be made when you buy a house. Make sure you have enough money available.

Legal Fees

Buyer's Solicitor
There is no fixed scale of solicitor's fees. As many buyers are anxious to budget as tightly as possible, solicitors nevertheless do

their best to quote a fee at the beginning of a transaction. At the time of preparing the present edition (autumn 1984) new projects are under discussion: the most hopeful, from a house-buyer's point of view, are probably those aimed at providing lists of houses, mortgages and legal services all under one roof. Buyers will probably get more expert help from solicitors running a property centre than from a commercially run property centre or a building society employing a solicitor. If you are paying a solicitor to look after your interests you want to be the one to whom he is responsible. If his boss is a building society or an estate agent you may, rightly or wrongly, wonder whose interests he is looking after. The staid image of building societies has recently suffered when they recommended types of mortgage to borrowers which were more in their own interests than in the interest of the borrower. In a few years there will be a new breed of semi-professionals, the 'licensed conveyancers', who will have some of the qualifications of a solicitor. It is too early to know what service they will offer and at what cost.

In the meantime, it is important not to be dazzled by the promise of low conveyancing costs. When you get a quotation make sure that it includes:

legal fees of buying;
legal fees for mortgage;
VAT on legal fees;
search fees;
Land Registry fees*;
stamp duties*;
any other fees.

The next few pages explain which of these fees apply to your house.

The legal fees of buying are generally somewhere below 1 per cent of the house price. But, since the amount of work to be done does not depend only on the price of the house, the percentage may well be lower for a more expensive house than for a cheaper one. Also, some solicitors will cut their fee to the minimum to give you a low quotation. They will obviously not be able to spend as much

---

* Not payable on every house (see pp. 64–5).

time on your particular problems – an owner who hustles you or who delays, a completion date which needs changing at the last moment – as the firm which allows itself a more generous margin. Some publicity has been given to the computerization of conveyancing. This should help to avoid spelling errors and to shorten routine work, but I doubt whether it will have much effect on the things worth paying for: the listening ear, professional advice and solutions to your particular problems.

As a general rule, the lawyer dealing with a house with unregistered title has to do more work and to take greater responsibility: he has to guarantee that all is well, whereas a registered title is guaranteed by the State. To give an example: H.M. Land Registry knows the name of the owner of every piece of registered land in the country, thus making it easy for your lawyer to find out whether you are buying from the real owner. With unregistered land this can be difficult: it is always possible for a crook to type out a deed showing himself to be the owner of Buckingham Palace, but you would not be safe to buy Buckingham Palace on the strength of that deed!

Apart from seeing to it that you buy from the right person, your solicitor has to make sure that you buy the right house and that you will be able to use it for the purpose for which you want it. A house on a new estate, though the title may be registered, tends to attract a great deal of paper – Deeds of Covenant, Deeds of Variation, Policies of Indemnity, Memorandum and Articles of Association, Planning Permission, Assignment of National Housebuilding Agreement, to name but a few. Some new housing developments change the neighbourhood completely: three old houses may easily become twenty-nine new flats – if you buy one of them you want to be assured that you will be able to enjoy it in peace. All this needs time, skill and care on the part of your solicitor, which may be reflected in the fees.

Mortgagee's Solicitor

Anyone lending money on mortgage will first want a solicitor to make sure that all is well with the title to the house. Here is your chance to save money. Find out from your solicitors for which building societies they act and try to get a mortgage from one of them. A solicitor acting for the building society *and* for the borrower will charge only this agreed fee for the mortgage work, although he takes responsibility to the buyer and to the society. Remember that this reduced scale holds good only if (1) your solicitor acts for you *and* for the building society, (2) your mortgage is £25,000 or less, and (3) house-buying and mortgage happen at the same time. You have to pay higher legal fees if you take a mortgage after buying the house (e.g. to build an extension) or if you buy without a solicitor (e.g. if you work through an unqualified conveyancing firm or if you do the legal work yourself).

Building society's legal fees (add VAT)

Mortgage:	£10,000	£20,000	£30,000
Legal fee: (repayment mortgage)	£52·50	£67·50	£75·00
Legal fee: (endowment mortgage)	£65·63	£84·38	£93·75

Insurance companies and banks also lend money on mortgage. They may suggest that you employ their solicitors to act for you. This is neither necessarily in your own best interest, nor will the reduced building society scale apply. Moral: talk to your solicitor before you apply for a mortgage; you may be able to save one set of fees.

Building Society Inspection Fee

No building society lends money unless its surveyor has seen the house and advised on whether the house will sell and repay your mortgage should you default. Fees depend on the price of the house, not on the amount you want to borrow, and vary slightly between societies.

Here are some typical examples, exclusive of VAT:

Price of house:	£10,000	£15,000	£20,000	£30,000
Fee:	£21	£31	£36	£46

Land Registry Fees

As soon as you have bought a house with unregistered title in an area of compulsory registration (more about this on pages 140–41) all the title deeds have to be sent to the Land Registry for the preparation of a land certificate (or charge certificate). Council houses bought by sitting tenants under the Housing Act 1980 must be registered, wherever they may be.

Land Registry fee on first registration:

Price of house:	£15,000	£20,000	£25,000	£30,000	£40,000
Land Registry fee:	£24	£30	£39	£45	£60

Where the title to the house is already registered, the land or charge certificate is sent to the Land Registry so that the new owner's name can be entered.

Land Registry fee for dealing with a registered title:

Price of house:	£15,000	£20,000	£25,000	£30,000	£40,000
Land Registry fee:	£38	£48	£63	£73	£98

Stamp Duty

Normally there is no stamp duty on a house or flat bought for £30,000 or less. Houses or flats costing over £30,000 are subject to stamp duty at 1 per cent. Thus, on a house costing exactly £30,000 you pay no stamp duty, but at £30,100 the stamp duty is £301.

Stamp on purchase deed

Price:	£15,000	£25,000	£35,000	£45,000
Duty:	nil	nil	£350	£450

There may be additional stamp duty if you are buying a house on a new lease (see below).

One reason why your solicitor is likely to collect all these fees from you before the house purchase is completed is that there are strict time limits. If documents are not stamped or sent to the Land Registry in time there are penalties to pay and you lose protection.

Stamp Duty on a New Lease

Let us suppose you buy a new flat for £15,000, with a lease for 120 years at a ground rent of £25 for the first thirty years (which is all you are likely to be concerned about as you intend to stay only a few years), the rent doubling every thirty years thereafter.

There is no stamp duty on the £15,000 (see above). But you have to pay stamp duty on the average rent (£93·75) calculated over the whole period of the lease.

To give some examples:

Stamp duty

Average yearly rent	£10	£50	£100
Lease for 99 years	£1·20	£6·00	£12·00
Lease for over 100 years	£2·40	£12·00	£24·00

Beware of an average yearly rent of more than £300. It attracts stamp duty on the purchase price, however low.

There is also an additional Land Registry fee. Though this is calculated at the highest possible rent under the lease, the extra fee is small. A rent of up to £200 means a fee of £2.

Other Fees

There will be other, minor, fees. There is a search fee to be paid to the local authority, probably £12·30, and there can be searches in the Land Charges Registry at 50p per name. Some solicitors charge separately for postage and telephones, others include these in their fees. Allow also for VAT.

Going through the above points you can check whether you can afford to buy the house of your choice.

Tom Jones's list of expenses looks something like this:

House price £28,000
Mortgage   £25,000
Title – registered
Purchaser's solicitor acting for building society

Capital	£3,000
Building society inspection fee	£15 + V A T
Solicitor's fee for house estimated at	£150 + V A T
Solicitor's fee for mortgage	£72·50 + V A T
Land Registry fee	£68
Stamp duty	nil

Allow another £30 for search fees and incidentals
Add cost of removal
Add cost of survey

The cost to Bella, the freelance, if she decided to buy, would be higher in spite of a similar capital contribution. This is because she cannot at present get all she wants on an ordinary building society mortgage. She might therefore try through a broker. If an insurance broker can raise the mortgage for her, she will probably get two mortgages – a building society one based on her income well over a year ago and a second, more expensive mortgage. The whole would probably have to be covered by an endowment policy, though if she is lucky only the second 'top up policy' will be made a condition for the loan. The insurance policy will have to be assigned to the lender as security for the repayment of the loan. An insurance broker will probably charge no further fee. A mortgage broker would charge a fee which is at his discretion. It is impossible to give a precise estimate of what Bella's fees would be, but she must ask, first the broker, then the solicitor, as she goes along and before she commits herself. Very roughly, her immediate expenses would come under these headings:

Capital
Inspection fee
Own solicitor's fees

Mortgagees' solicitor's fees
(Broker's fees)
First insurance premium
Fees on assignment of insurance policy
Land Registry fees and other expenses: similar to Tom and May's.

Many people have no choice when to buy. An immigrant family, for example, will need a house as quickly as possible. Even if there is capital available in the family, it may be required for business.

To borrow, in spite of unusually high expense, may make good sense; but, before you commit yourself, do make an estimate.

Your estimated cost

Capital		
Building society inspection fee*		
Solicitor's fee*	house	
	mortgage	
Land Registry fee	house	
Stamp duty	house	
Other fees		
Removal*		
Survey*		
	———	
	£	
	———	

* Add V A T to all these items.

If at this point you come to the view that you simply cannot afford the kind of home you had in mind, what can you do? Here are some ideas to try:

(1) Look in a different road
            in a different district
            for a smaller house
            for an older house.

(2) Look for a better-paid job.

(3) Try other building societies.

(4) Consider whether you can add to your income in other ways (e.g. by working extra time, doing part-time minicab driving, cleaning or decorating).

(5) Consider adding to your present house instead of moving.

(6) Try to find a flat under a shared ownership scheme (more about this on p. 128).

(7) Look into the possibility of renting, using a housing association, or sharing with somebody else (for most of us these last three possibilities are not very hopeful).

Perhaps you feel you can afford the house and the running of it, but you cannot raise a big enough mortgage. If so, can you increase your capital by doing some extra work as suggested above, or by letting a room, or by living with mother for a while? These, I realize, are desperate remedies, but they are only temporary and they will allow you to put money by – if you are strong-minded.

Or you could try a mortgage broker, to see whether he can get a bigger loan for you, but look carefully at any increased offers. Unconventional lenders often charge a good deal more than ordinary building societies. If the loan means higher monthly payments you may be worse off in the long run. As has been mentioned, many brokers charge a fee for introducing business or insist on your taking out an insurance policy which may or may not be useful to you.

The Cost of Running a Home

Mortgage Payments

All mortgages have one thing in common: regular payments by the borrower till the loan is paid back, with interest. The majority specify monthly or quarterly payments. If you yourself are paid monthly, you may find it most convenient to pay your mortgage monthly by banker's order. This is ideal if your firm pays direct into your bank. If it does not, remember to put enough money into the bank.

Payment by banker's order is easily arranged. Tell your bank

how much to pay, on what day of the month and to whom. It does
the rest. When interest rates change your monthly payments may
also change. Unless your bank has your authority to pay whatever
the building society demands, banker's orders may need altering
from time to time as interest rates change.

If you had to take out an expensive second mortgage or bank
loan it might be worth asking the building society after a time
whether it will increase your first mortgage to allow you to pay off
the bank loan. By this method your monthly payments can come
down a good way.

Ground Rent

In some parts of the country freehold houses attract a payment of
rent, usually called 'chief rent'. Leasehold houses and flats are
always liable to ground rent. Apart from these exceptions there is
no need to allow for rent.

Insurance

House
To insure the house against fire and other common risks is
common sense. When there is a mortgage on the house, the
lenders (building society, bank or insurance company) insist on
house insurance, usually through their agency. You should, however, be given a reasonable choice of insurance companies. When
the house or flat you buy is leasehold, the owner of the freehold
often makes the right to handle the insurance of the building a term
of the lease. The building society usually gives way and allows
the freeholder to insure. This is sensible: a leasehold house or flat is
usually one of several in the same block or road. If some flats are
damaged the insurance claim is more easily dealt with by one
insurance company than by several. House insurance premiums
are fairly reasonable, about £1·50 a year for every £1,000 insurance under a comprehensive policy. There is more about house
insurance in Chapter 13, 'Between Contract and Completion'.

Furniture, etc.

It is in your own interest to insure the contents of your house. It is also easy to forget, because no building society, solicitor or insurance agent is likely to push the right form in front of you at the right moment. The right moment is as soon as you own the stuff: it could be stolen or burnt the very next day. You can, but don't have to, insure with the company which insures your house. See what different insurance companies have to offer before you choose. Unless you are told differently, the ordinary contents policy covers your goods only for their value at the time of the disaster, which may be a good deal less than it costs to replace them. Therefore, go for an index-linked policy offering to replace your belongings, if you can afford it.

Many policies exclude money above £50 or £100 (unless you pay an extra premium); for a comparatively small additional premium you can also insure your jewellery, sports equipment, the contents of your freezer, etc.

Endowment or Top Up Insurance Policy

Ordinary life insurance is beyond the scope of this book. You may find, however, that you cannot get the mortgage you need to buy the house without taking out some kind of insurance maturing at the end of your mortgage or on your earlier death. Such policies can be expensive; get several quotations from different firms if you possibly can (see also 'Endowment Mortgage', pp. 44–8).

Mortgage Protection Policy

A mortgage protection policy costs a good deal less than an ordinary life policy, because its purpose is much more limited: it does no more than repay the mortgage if you should die before you have paid it off. If you survive to the end of the mortgage period, you stop paying insurance premiums, but you get nothing. For a slightly higher premium you can insure the mortgage plus a sum of money at the end of the mortgage term. This type of insurance is comparatively inexpensive, particularly if you are young when you take it out; at the same time it is a comfort in case the breadwinner should die. A form of mortgage protection policy is also used for part of the 'low cost' endowment insurance (p. 45).

Rates and Water Rate

Both depend on the rateable value of the house. The rateable value of any house can be discovered from the local authority. The current rate varies from year to year and depends on what the local authority needs that year for schools, parks, housing and all the other responsibilities of local government. A rate of 80p in the £ on a house with rateable value of £100 means a rate demand through your letterbox for 100 times 80p, or £80. For rating purposes the year begins on 1 April and soon after that date you will know how much to put by for rates for the next twelve months. Many people prefer to pay monthly.

The water rate is in some areas included in the same demand note, in others it is sent separately. It is a smaller payment, but, like the general rate, may vary from year to year.

Those with a low income may claim a reduction of rate. For details apply to the local authority.

There are other outgoings. How much you will have to allow for them depends partly on taste, partly on luck. In any case you should bear them in mind. Here are some examples:

Repairs

If you are wise you will have had the house surveyed (see Chapter 9, 'Surveyors') before you bought it and will have a rough idea of its condition. An old house bought at a low price will probably need more extensive repairs than a new one. You should know about the likelihood of settlement, the need for roof repairs and the presence of rot and woodworm, before you move. It is possible that the building society may specify repairs which have to be done before it will lend money on a house; it is more likely that it will hold back part of the mortgage money till these repairs have been carried out. Requirements of this kind are included in the mortgage offer, so that you can plan accordingly. Your surveyor may also be able to give you a rough idea of how much to allow for routine maintenance per year. In addition there are bound to be unexpected repairs, though some of these may be covered by insurance (see above).

Painting and papering the inside of the house will take more or less money depending on how often you decorate and whether you do the work yourself or have it done professionally. A room which is well lived in will probably need repainting every three years or so.

Service Charge

The lease of a flat in a modern block will probably say that major repairs and maintenance will be done for you and that you will have to share the cost. Sometimes central heating or hot water are provided in this way; or there may be a caretaker who cleans the stairs and looks after the garden. All such expenses are usually called 'service charge'. Ask the present owner how much he has had to pay each year and what his service charge includes. This will give you an idea of how much to allow under this heading. If the cost of major repairs to the building is included in the service charge you can allow a smaller sum under the heading 'repairs'.

Fares

As a rule, houses near the centre of a town are more expensive than those further out, though fashionable suburbs may be dearer than slummy houses further in. You may have to decide whether you prefer to spend more on a house near your place of work and less on fares, or the other way round. Bear in mind that fares tend to go up rather more frequently than mortgage rates, and allow for time spent on travelling to and from work.

If you travel by car, there is the question of a garage. If your house has no garage, will the car depreciate too fast? Opinions vary, and so do cars. Weigh against the price of renting a garage the possibility of having to pay parking fees, and possibly parking fines.

Shops, Domestic Help, etc.

Your cost of living goes up if you have an expensive journey to good shops, or if the shops near you are expensive. Prices can vary considerably even between one part of a suburb and another. The presence of a supermarket or two will probably mean shopping at reasonable prices.

Domestic help is not only more expensive but also more difficult to find in more 'select' areas. It is equally difficult to find in areas where there are many factories offering part-time employment for women. If you depend on the help of a charwoman this point is worth remembering.

Entertaining

The cost of your social life does not necessarily depend on the area where you live. A hermit can live independent of others. But the chances are that if everyone in the road has a Jaguar you may not long feel happy with your own Mini, and even if you do, your wife won't, and the children will most certainly wish to do just as everyone else in their school or street. It is worth peering through the neighbours' windows before finally deciding on the house. You may feel equally uncomfortable if yours is the Jaguar and the neighbours go about in elderly bone-shakers.

Jot down the figures as they come, and then work out how much to allow per month. For example, if rates are £150 per half-year, allow £25 per month; if fares are £1 a day and you work a five-day week, allow 22 working days per month, or £22.

Estimated cost of running your house

Mortgage	£	Total per month
(Ground rent or chief		
rent)	£	(per year)
Insurance		
House	£	per year
Contents	£	
Mortgage	£	

Rates	£	per half-year
Water rate	£	per half-year
Fares	£	per day/week
Repairs/Service charge	£	per year

If you are paid weekly, you may find it useful to make a weekly budget rather than a monthly one. But in any event, don't assume that because you have a little over in one month you will not need it during the following month.

Chapter 5

Estate Agents

You are unlikely to buy a house without at some point getting help from an estate agent.

If you have read the earlier chapters you will have begun house-hunting from the comfort of your home, reading small advertisements in 'Houses for Sale' columns of different newspapers. The majority of these advertisements are put in by estate agents. You will probably write to some of the advertisers for further details (see p. 25 for some words of warning and specimen letters).

You will again meet estate agents on your visits to the area where you are looking for a house. As you emerge from the railway station your eye will almost certainly fall on one or more agents' shop windows. Estate agents are attracted to stations like pins to a magnet. Look in the shop windows. Even if you do not see what you want, a visit can do no harm. Many agents are happy to put every inquirer on their list.

The agent will ask a number of questions, such as how much you want to spend on the house, whether you want a mortgage and for how much, how many rooms you want, whether you need a garage and whether you have a particular area in mind. You may think all manner of other points more important, but these are the ones that matter to agents and will decide what information they are going to send you in the future. In my experience it is pretty useless to tell an agent, for example, that you want a house to which another room could be added, or one facing in a particular direction – his indexing system is rarely geared to picking out this kind of information.

The amount of mortgage will have much to do with the kind of house which agents will bring to your notice. You might enjoy living in a converted windmill, but you won't be able to borrow 95 per cent of the purchase price on mortgage for anything other than a conventionally built house or flat.

While you are with him, the agent may suggest a few houses which you can visit then and there. He may even offer to take you. This is particularly useful if your time is limited. No reputable agent will ask you to sign any document, so regard any suggestion of this kind with suspicion. Agents are often very helpful merely in the hope of showing you the house of your choice; you are under no obligation either to buy or to pay them a fee even if you travel round with them all afternoon – though naturally you cannot expect free transport all the time. On the way you may come across the boards of other agents, advertising houses for sale. Get in touch with some of them and ask for particulars of other houses. The agent who shows you round may be willing to get such information for you. In many towns agents help one another in this way.

If the agent has nothing suitable to offer on the spot, he will nevertheless put your name on his mailing list. If you have to come from some distance to look at houses he may be able to arrange for you to see several on your next visit. In the meantime you will be receiving sheaves of literature from him if this is a quiet time of year. If you are house-hunting in the middle of a season of panic-buying, on the other hand, all the running will have to be made by you. Concentrate on one or two agents, or you will lose your sanity – and keep your eyes open for other possibilities, as suggested on pages 25–6.

If at all feasible, get familiar with the problems of house-hunting during the quiet season.

The language used by estate agents can itself be a problem. Some agents indulge in amusing description, making ordinary houses sound fun to live in. This is all to the good, so long as you remember that you will have to live in the ordinary house long after you have forgotten the fanciful description. The majority of agents use words which the house-hunter may at first find bewildering. How, for the money at his disposal, can he possibly expect anything as grand as a 'residence with two reception rooms and a well-kept garden'? Before the vision of his stately-home-to-be runs away with him and he rushes out to buy, he would do well to keep his head and to begin to understand some of the language used by estate agents.

There is little difference between a 'house', a 'residence' and a 'property'. A 'residence' tends to be slightly larger and draughtier than a 'property', though a 'bijou residence' is likely to be very small indeed. A 'period style' residence probably means either mock Georgian or mock Tudor. 'Ready for modernization', 'old-world charm' or 'fully modernized' should warn you that the building needs a careful survey. 'Panoramic view' may mean 'very windy'; 'close to city centre' could be very noisy. A semi-detached house has three outside walls to look after; a detached house has four. Detached houses, even if built close together, tend to fetch higher prices, terraced houses (attached on both sides) tend to go for less, except for modern 'town houses', or houses in a genuine period terrace. Bungalows do not usually present any mortgage problems, but houses with part possession do. Building societies do not usually take kindly to a house part of which is occupied by a sitting tenant.

The great majority of houses offered for sale are built on two floors. Agents usually call any room on the first floor a bedroom and on the ground floor a reception room. 'Reception room' does not mean that it will be large enough for receptions; it is merely a word for 'living room', though an upstairs room may have a pleasant view, get more sun and make an altogether better living room than those on the ground floor. An 'integral garage' cannot necessarily be reached from inside the house. A 'master bedroom' indicates that there is at least one other bedroom, even smaller. A 'double bedroom' will be large enough to hold a double bed. In some modern flats, however, there may not be enough space to get in and out of that bed on both sides, or to add items of luxury such as a wardrobe. A built-in wardrobe might be worth two feet of space, particularly if it has sliding doors. The agent's particulars will probably include approximate measurements for each room. Bear in mind that size alone does not always give a clear picture. Some new dwellings are marvels of planning and use space most ingeniously. This could mean that you could do without a lot of furniture, because much is built in, or that you can make do with a place smaller than you had thought possible because, for example, the built-in breakfast counter extends to make a dining table. But not every modern house is well planned. 'Bathroom en suite' could mean that you cannot reach a WC except by going through the main bedroom. For such a house you need a second lavatory.

Modern kitchens are often referred to as 'kitchenettes'; a room with nothing but a sink is called a 'scullery' in an old house and a 'utility room' in a new house. A 'patio' may mean a delightful paved garden area, or a dreary back yard. A 'study' will probably be designed for a studious dwarf.

A word about flats and maisonettes. 'Maisonnette' is French for a 'small house'; in modern English the word is usually spelt with one 'n' and betokens never more than part of a house. Neither 'flat' nor 'maisonette' is a very exact term, though most agents and property developers talk of a 'flat' if it is reached through a common entrance, shared by the occupiers of other flats. A modern 'maisonette', on the other hand, is usually reached by its own staircase if on the first floor, and direct from the outside if on the ground floor. Older maisonettes are sometimes on two floors, modern maisonettes more often on one floor. A 'studio flat' will have only one room plus (with luck) a kitchen, bath and WC. A 'penthouse' is high up and very expensive. Most building societies are as willing to lend on modern flats and maisonettes as on modern houses. You may find it harder to borrow on an older house or on a flat built by dividing up a one-family house, particularly if you want to contribute only a small percentage of the price.

Agents' leaflets often give the rateable value of a house and the annual rate (e.g. RV £250, rate 80p in the £). From this you can work out how much to allow for rates if you buy that house. The leaflet will end with a price. Whether the house is worth its price is something on which a surveyor can advise.

The price, except of a new house, is rarely final. Most owners start by asking the price they hope to get, but settle for a little less if they were too optimistic. Some ask for more, knowing that they will probably have to make some reduction. The price of a new house is not as a rule open to bargaining. Developers sometimes lower the price of houses to speed up sales, but rarely at the behest of would-be buyers. The agent will advise on whether a lower offer is likely to be well received. The fact that he has the owner's interest at heart does not mean that he will not help you. He is anxious to get a sale at a reasonable figure rather than to hang on in the hope of squeezing another few pounds out of a buyer who may not materialize for months. If you are seriously interested in the house, there is no harm in putting in a lower offer.

Tom Jones's brother did just this. He liked a maisonette which he thought a little expensive. He offered £1,000 less than the advertised price, but the agent told him that another offer at that price had been turned down. The agent talked to the owner on the telephone and suggested a reduction of £600 as no one else had shown serious interest in the maisonette. The owner said 'Try to get a little more'. In the end the price was reduced by £450. All sides felt they had done well. The owner had bought the maisonette several years earlier at less than half the sale price and had made a profit. Jones felt pleased because he had beaten down the seller, and the agent was pleased because he had earned his commission. There is no fixed scale. Many agents charge $2\frac{1}{2}$ per cent of the selling price plus V A T. Sole agents charge less. Estate agents' commission is usually paid by the seller of the house, not by the buyer. If, therefore, you found your house, not through an agent, but by answering the owner's advertisement, you might be able to get a slight reduction in price. You can point out that by selling to you he saved a good deal of money (possibly $2\frac{1}{2}$ to 3 per cent of the price) in estate agents' fees.

People with very different qualifications carry on business as estate agents. An agent may have qualified after a course in estate management and years of professional training; he may specialize in selling houses and goods by auction, in letting flats, in collecting rents, or in making valuations. Some agents are less concerned with professional skills than with the business of selling houses, with the result that there are firms without a single professionally qualified member. This is no reflection on their skill or their ability to help a house-hunter.

Whatever his professional qualifications, or even if he has no professional qualifications, an estate agent can be extremely useful to the house-buyer. For one thing, he is likely to know more about houses for sale in his area than anyone else. In some areas all agents co-operate and exchange lists, so that it is enough to see one in order to hear of all the houses in the district. But this is by no means universal, and it is quite a good idea for you to visit two or three agents in one area in order to hear about as many houses as possible. At the same time be warned and do not buy merely on the strength of a first impression.

The very friendliness and helpfulness of an estate agent some-times leads buyers astray. The agent is employed by the *owner* of a house to sell that house. He must not give you a misleading description of the house, but it is not an agent's function to warn a buyer of its defects. Indeed, he may well be failing in his duty to the seller if he did warn you. It is therefore up to you to be wary.

The agent may also suggest a building society which may give you a mortgage. Although this can be helpful advice, you might be able to save money by checking with your solicitor whether he acts for that building society.

There may be other ways of cutting down on your costs. You could try to find a house through one of the new 'shops' exhibiting lists of houses for sale, if there is one in your preferred area. They can be run by local authorities or commercially. The seller saves by selling through them rather than through an estate agent, and some of that saving might be passed on to you.

There may be a property centre in your area offering house, mortgage and conveyancing, all for one combined fee. These centres are too new (autumn 1984) for me to say how good they are. The idea as such is splendid, but check what is on offer and what it costs. Remember: (1) a buyer should not have to pay anything to an estate agent; and (2) the only fee you have to pay for the mortgage is the building society inspection fee (see pp. 63–4). Therefore, apart from (2), you should be paying only the fees set out on pp. 60–65. Make sure you get what you are paying for.

Part 2

The House You Want

Chapter 6

Meeting the Owner and Making Sure

Before you meet *the* owner, you will have met a great many owners of a great many houses. This is as it should be: you would be unwise to buy the first house you see without also inspecting others. However good this first house may look to you, take time to read local papers and to visit the area, as recommended in earlier chapters. Be particularly wary of two points:

The price: Although this house may be a lot cheaper than a similar house you saw earlier in the week in another area, do not jump to the conclusion that you are on to a bargain. House prices vary extraordinarily, not only from one part of the country to another, but even from one part of the city to another. Even within the same suburb you may find two similar houses offered at different prices. Before you rush in to buy the lower priced house, make sure that it really is a bargain: consider its age and condition, and, above all, compare it with other houses in the immediate neighbourhood.

The future: If the house really seems a bargain, check that its future is relatively safe. Maybe the price has come down because of a road-widening scheme, or because there are plans for a new airfield round the corner. A visit to the local town hall and to the local pub will probably yield information on these points. Tee-totallers might try a local shop – not of course self-service; a nice, slow, old-fashioned shop lends itself to conversation and is often visited by old residents who will, at the drop of a hint, shake their heads about what the neighbourhood is coming to. This is precisely what you want to know: what *is* the neighbourhood coming to? But, as with pub information, take it with a pinch of salt and check with the local council. The chief use of local gossip is that it gives you an idea of what questions to ask of the council.

Gaining experience involves not only looking at local papers but also walking round many houses. After a time you will be able to recognize within two minutes the house you do *not* want. You are then in a difficulty. Should you tour the house, wasting a lot of time, yours and the owner's, and leave, mumbling 'I'll let you know'? Or should you take a look at the house and retire hurriedly, leaving the owner waiting and wondering?

To my mind it is a reasonable compromise to inspect at least two rooms to make sure your impression was correct, and then to end the inspection with a reasonable excuse which will not deflate the owner too much. 'I'm afraid it will be too difficult to get my grandmother's wheelchair up the stairs' is better than 'The view from the back window is too depressing for words'. Remember that the owner is human. If you have made an appointment and cannot keep it, let him know. He may have stayed at home to show you the house, or he may have gone there specially to meet you: the poor man deserves an apology, even if you do not like his house, or are too weary to make the trip.

Let us assume you have reached the dizzy point when you like the house and the view from the house, and it comes within the price range you can afford.

Take another long cool look.

Are the windows double-glazed? Do they open easily? Is the attic insulated? How about draughts? If there is central heating, is it in every room?

Perhaps the house is beautifully painted and papered, all floors covered with fitted carpets and vinyl tiles, the whole thing spotless and well cared for. How marvellous to move in without having to decorate! But it is as well to allow for the possibility that the house was newly decorated in order to hide cracks under the paper and rot under the tiles. A surveyor will be able to tell.

Conversely, do not be put off by the owner's ghastly taste; old paint and ugly wallpaper can be removed. And his awful curtains and greasy mats will leave with him. It is quite possible that you will be able to buy the house at a much lower price than one that was recently dolled up. The owner may have paid all of two thousand pounds for the house some thirty years ago and feel that he is making a splendid profit.

Whether or not you share the owner's tastes, try to imagine the house with all furniture removed, and refurnish it in your mind. Imagine your family moving round the house. The back room, dark now because the curtains are drawn and the sun is at the front, will get the afternoon sun and would take Granny's large wardrobe. The washing machine could go to the right of the sink. The stairs are a little steep for your toddler, but he won't be a toddler much longer and you can fix a gate at the top of the stairs.

It is a little difficult if, while you are busy imagining, you also have to cope with a talkative owner, bent on explaining every advantage of the house. You may find it best to listen to him on your first round, and then ask him to let you go round once more. If he insists on tagging along, ignore his further remarks and concentrate. You can come out of your trance every now and then and explain with an apologetic smile: 'I am so sorry, I did not hear what you said. I am trying very hard to remember everything about the house so that I can tell my wife/husband all about it. Do you mind if I continue?'

Do not allow your irritation with the owner to colour your impression of the house. He will go, taking with him his noisy children and his revolting pets. It is not safe to assume that, because he is awful, your new neighbours are going to be like him. He may have been the scourge of the neighbourhood and the neighbours may all be watching and praying behind their curtains that he will go and you will buy. Equally, do not let a charming owner with impeccable taste and beautiful furniture persuade you to buy an unsuitable house. He too will go, leaving you to do the best you can with your sagging three-piece suite and the carpet with the hole at the centre.

Use all your senses. Do not only look at the house, listen for traffic, factories, schools, railways, birds, music. You will get some idea of what to expect. If possible, pay several calls at different times of the day. Your nose also has its part to play. The delicious smell of roses or lilac may give you a quite illusory air of luxury. And the fusty smell of cats, or not enough windows open, may put you off. (On this I speak with feeling: my family refused a house because the owner bred, and did not clean up after, a very large number of cats. Nothing I could say persuaded them that the cats would leave and the smell evaporate.) But a bad smell may betoken bad drains or dry rot – a surveyor should be able to tell the difference!

It is important to use your imagination when looking at a house, but it is as well to keep your feet on the ground. Not every old cowshed converts into a dream cottage. Many derelict buildings are in that state because it would cost too much to put them right. Not every old house lends itself to modernization: some are the wrong shape for modern furniture, and the money it would take to convert is better employed in buying a more expensive house in the first place. On the other hand, four sound walls and a good roof may give a lot of scope for improvement without financial ruin. If you are thinking of converting a shed, church, school or railway station, get a builder or architect to look at it before you commit yourself. Also, find out whether you could get a local authority grant.

Some Pitfalls

Your Offer Letter

When you have made up your mind to buy the house, you will want the owner to know as soon as possible – indeed, you are probably anxious in case he sells to somebody else. By all means tell him you would like to buy his house, that you are at once applying for a mortgage and that he will be hearing from your solicitor. But take care: Chapter 12 explains in more detail that neither the buyer nor the seller of a house is bound to go on with the sale until they exchange contracts. It also explains why you cannot safely enter into a contract till you know a good deal more about the house. You must therefore be careful not to bind yourself unwittingly. Your letter to the owner, however friendly, may amount to the 'written evidence' which in law can make the difference between a tentative offer and a binding contract. Whether you talk to the owner or whether you write, make it clear that your offer is SUBJECT TO CONTRACT. You could write something like this:

Letter to owner

Dear Mr
  Thank you for letting me see the house again on Sunday. I liked it very much and hope to make a formal offer for it. I am going to see the building society tomorrow, and have made an appointment with my solicitor for Thursday. I am asking him to write to you, or if you can let me have the name and address of your own solicitor before Thursday I shall ask mine to get in touch with yours.

Yours sincerely,

This letter, without committing you, tells the owner that you are serious about his house. In times of shortage you can say the same thing more emphatically – but you must still take care not to commit yourself. If you have prepared your visit, you might be able to write:

  As I told you, our building society has already promised us a mortgage in principle. I am asking them today how soon I can expect the money. I am also telling my solicitor to go ahead and shall be in touch with you as soon as the mortgage offer comes in. In the meantime, I am sending off a preliminary deposit.

It may be that you want to explore whether the owner will reduce the price and do not want to go to a solicitor till you know whether you will be able to afford the house. In that case, if you follow the wording of the next letter fairly closely (leaving out what does not apply), you are safe. But do not use phrases like 'I am offering', or 'Will you take'.

Letter to owner

Dear Mr
  Thank you for letting us see the house again on Sunday. We liked it very much and hope to make a formal offer. Would you consider

£   , subject to contract, the price to include the vinyl in bathroom, kitchen and hall, and all light fittings?*

I am sorry I cannot offer the full price, but as you know, the house will need repainting and the bathroom modernizing. If you are prepared to sell the house to me, please give me the name and address of your solicitors. I shall ask my solicitors to get in touch with them.

Yours sincerely,

If you saw the house through an estate agent, there is no need to write to the owner at all. Telephone the agent instead and ask him to contact the owner. You can at the same time mention to him any defects which you feel might persuade the owner to lower his price. Even without defect, the owner may well be prepared to lower his price; most house prices are fixed with the idea of dropping a few hundred pounds if need be. If there is no urgency, you could write:

Letter to an estate agent

Dear Sir,

re: 14 Chestnut Avenue

Would you please find out whether the owner is willing to sell this house for £   , subject to contract. I think the price at which it is offered is rather high: the house needs repainting and the bathroom is very old-fashioned. I have spoken to the   Building Society who are willing to consider a mortgage application. As soon as I hear from you that my offer is acceptable, I shall make a formal application. My solicitors are Messrs Stokes & Stokes of   .

Yours faithfully,

If you have already been to a solicitor and discussed the purchase with him, you can ask your solicitor to put forward the offer. This is particularly convenient if you are dealing direct with the owner, without an estate agent. Write to the solicitor:

Dear Mr Stokes,

Would you please offer £   for 14 Chestnut Avenue, Bursledon, the house about which I saw you last week. The owner is Mr   . I answered his advertisement in the local paper; there is no agent involved. I do not know the name of his solicitor.

---

*Or whatever else the owner has told you he would include in the sale for no extra payment. If nothing was said, leave this part of the sentence out.

If he is prepared to sell at my price I shall send a surveyor and then apply for a mortgage.

(Or: Could you in the meantime please suggest a building society which might lend me £   .) Please let me know when I should pay a deposit.

                    Yours sincerely,

If you have not yet been to a solicitor, now is the time to go.

The Deposit

You may feel that, to stop the owner from selling the house to anybody else, you should as quickly as possible press money into his hands. This impulse is human, but the owner is not bound to reserve the house for you even if you pay a deposit. His solicitor, once he has sent a contract to your solicitor, will not normally deal with a second applicant for the house without first sending out a warning. You cannot, however, rely on this. Therefore, do not pay a deposit direct to the owner. If you do and the sale falls through, you might have difficulty in claiming your deposit back. If you cannot resist the impulse to pay a deposit, pay through a solicitor. He will make sure that you can get it back.

Above all, do not get carried away. Do not start buying carpets or furniture. You cannot be certain of getting the house till contracts have been exchanged. If the sale falls through, even though it is no fault of yours and much to your disappointment, you can get no compensation from the owner. He is not responsible for your carpets, your hurt feelings, your building society fees or your legal costs.

This seems enormously unjust till you find yourself in the position of one of Tom's friends. Roger had fondly hoped to buy a house to go with his new job. Then he heard the new job did not offer the bright future he had been led to expect. He stayed put in his old job and his old house. The owner of the new house had been waiting for many weeks, lost the house he had hoped to buy and spent several hundred pounds on finding another house for his family. All this because he had relied on Roger to buy his house. Yet Roger owed him no compensation.

Gazumping

In recent years this principle of not being bound to buy or sell a house till contracts are exchanged has given more offence to buyers than sellers. A house-owner may quite enjoy showing you his property today and agreeing a price with you. He can show it to somebody else tomorrow and settle for a higher price. Till one of you signs and exchanges contracts with the owner, no one is under any liability to go on.

If you relied on the owner to sell to you, paid for a survey, applied for a mortgage, consulted a solicitor and, after some weeks, are told he wants more money or is selling to somebody else, you are understandably cross. No one has found a solution to this problem, though solicitors have at least made it a rule not to deal with more than one would-be buyer without letting the other know. You are, therefore, fairly safe in assuming that you are the only buyer, till your solicitor gets a letter telling him the owner is dealing with somebody else.

If you are trying to buy at a time when everyone seems to be frantically house-hunting, it is best not to bargain with the owner. Offer him the price he is asking and suggest he give you a clear run for a few weeks. Then, try to persuade your building society to write a letter saying they will grant you a mortgage, even though there may be some delay before you can actually get the money. Armed with this letter you can ask your bank whether it will lend you the mortgage money for a short time.

You can also ask your solicitor whether you yourself can do anything to speed up the local authority search, *but* do not get carried away. Work out whether the extra cost, risk and excitement are worth it, or whether you might do better to wait for the fever to subside, as it probably will in late summer or autumn.

It is impossible to give reliable advice on this thorny subject. House prices can rise very rapidly at times, but such periods are usually followed by a lull or even a slight drop in prices.

If you are not pushed for time and if you have a house to sell as well as wishing to buy, you will probably have a less frustrating time if you wait. First-time buyers, on the other hand, may fear that prices will rise much faster than their savings. They might consider camping out to queue for a newly built house; prices tend to be fixed and gazumping is cut out.

Some builders of new housing estates offer an option: for a payment of, say, £100 the house is reserved for you for a period at a fixed price. If you buy, the £100 becomes part of the purchase money. If you don't (e.g. because you can't get a mortgage), you lose the deposit. This is not to be recommended unless you are virtually certain that you can buy the house, but is possibly less frustrating than the uncertainty connected with the other forms of purchasing.

At whatever time you buy, make it a rule not to discuss business with the owner. Visit him by all means, though not too often or he will worry and think that you are in doubt about whether you really want his house. Oddly enough, you are expected to make up your mind about a house, where you may spend the best part of your life, after the most cursory visits. The owner does not think this odd: he still regards the house as his and wants to go on living there undisturbed till it is sold. He will tolerate, with as much grace as he can muster, visits from surveyors. The rest is better done by correspondence, via estate agents or solicitors.

Chapter 7

Help! You Need a Solicitor

Try to find solicitors in the very early stages of your house-hunt – you may need them in a hurry.

The best idea is to go back to a firm which has acted for you before and did a good job. It does not matter if this was not in connection with house-buying.

If you have not been to a solicitor before, ask for recommendations from your family and friends. Lawyers are trained to be discreet, and your affairs will be private even if the same solicitor acts for other members of the family.

If you still have not found a lawyer, you could ask your local bank, the building society or estate agent to recommend one, or ask the local Citizens' Advice Bureau or the Law Society. The last two will not recommend a particular firm, but both can give you a list of local solicitors.

As yet, no 'licensed conveyancers' have passed the necessary examinations to act on your behalf. When they do, their qualifications will be far more limited than those of solicitors.

I suggest you fix an appointment with a properly qualified solicitor as soon as you come up against any of the following points:

you do not know which kind of mortgage is best for you – see Chapter 3;

you have a choice of sources from which you can borrow and cannot decide which is most suitable for you;

the building society cold-shoulders you – see Chapter 3;

you are asked to pay a deposit – see Chapter 8, 'The Deposit';

you are thinking of buying a lease, or a house with part possession;

you are a sitting tenant and are offered your house;

you are a council tenant and are offered your house – the council will offer you a mortgage but its terms should be compared with other mortgage possibilities before you decide;

somebody else is after the house you badly want.

Some of these points need explaining.

Where to Borrow

Ask the solicitors where best to apply for a mortgage. They will know who favours your kind of house. Also, if they can recommend a building society on whose panel their name is included, you will save money. How? Before they lend, building societies must make sure that the house on which they are lending is a good risk; they are handing out money entrusted to them by people who want to see it back, with interest. They must investigate in three directions: (1) will the borrower be good for the money lent to him; can he afford the monthly payments; has he met his obligations in the past? (2) is the house soundly built and worth lending on? If it falls down before the mortgage is repaid, or if it is worth less than the amount of the loan, it might have to be sold at a loss and the building society might not see its money back: and (3) is the legal title good?

The first point is assessed by the building society itself. For the second it employs a surveyor. The third is the solicitors' problem. Some building societies employ lawyers on their staff to deal with the legal side, but many authorize selected firms of solicitors to act for them. They become 'panel solicitors'. Your solicitors will almost certainly be on the panel of several societies, and your legal fees will be smaller if you can get a mortgage through one of these solicitors.

As your solicitors must in any event make sure that you get a good title, they can give the building society the answer it needs without much extra work. Your fees are correspondingly lower than if a second solicitor has to do the job from scratch.

Buying a Lease

A house offered on a long lease is probably as valuable as a comparable freehold house. The tail end of what was once a long lease could be a bargain if it carried with it the right to buy the freehold; it could become an expensive nightmare if at the end of the lease you had to do all the repairs left undone by previous owners.

How long is a 'long lease'? In law, any lease over twenty-one years is 'long', but you may need a very much more extensive term. Any lease which has less than seventy years to run should lead to a quick telephone call to your solicitor before you commit yourself in any way.

If you are buying a *flat* it will almost certainly be leasehold. This is no disadvantage. There is much more about flats in Chapter 10, 'Buying a Flat or a New House'. If you are thinking of buying a leasehold *house*, read on.

A freehold house is yours forever, a leasehold one only until the lease runs out. Building societies love freehold houses, and house-hunters who want to borrow as much money as possible are wise to look at freehold houses or very long leaseholds. The difference from the house-buyer's point of view is that a leasehold house will cost rent each year. This rent, known as ground rent, tends to be very small and is not usually a great worry. Much more important is the fact that, in theory at least, at the end of the lease the house goes back to the owner of the ground. Leasehold houses therefore are worth less as time goes on, whereas freehold houses tend to go up in value. Building societies do not usually lend on a house with a lease of less than forty years to run; some put the limit as low as sixty years.

But, thanks to the Leasehold Reform Act 1967, more and more leaseholds are capable of becoming freeholds. If you are interested in a leasehold house, find out whether the present owner has the right to buy the freehold. That right could be transferred to you. The house will be worth more with the right to buy than without it.

To benefit from the Act, the would-be buyer of the freehold must fulfil a number of requirements:

(1) The house must be his main residence. The majority of people consider one 'residence' all they can manage. But if for example you have a weekend cottage in the country and a house in town, the town house is the one to which the Act applies. Once you sell that and retire to your country cottage, the cottage becomes your main (or only) residence, and the Act applies to the cottage.

(2) You must have lived there for at least three years. This period can either be the three years just past, or three out of the last ten.

(3) During the material years you must have occupied the house either as owner or as a member of the owner's family. The owner's widow, for example, need not wait till she herself has owned the house for three years. She can use the Act three years after her husband bought the lease.

(4) The rateable value of the house on 23 March 1965 must have been £200 or less in England or Wales (or £400 or less in London). If it is higher the Act does not apply.

(5) The ground rent must be less than two thirds of that rateable value. If it is higher, the Act does not apply.

(6) The lease must, originally, have been for more than twenty-one years. This does not mean that there must be a lot of it left when you buy.

The owner of a house to which all these points apply can usually – there are a few exceptions – insist on buying the freehold at a reasonable figure, or, if he prefers, get an extension of the lease for fifty years, at a higher rent.

How does this affect you, the house-hunter? Obviously you cannot insist on buying, or getting an extension of, the lease till you have lived in the house for three years. You may feel inclined to take a chance, move in and buy after that time. This is a little risky – the law may be changed, and you do not know how much the cost will be in three years – and should not be undertaken without advice from a solicitor or surveyor.

You could try a different solution: ask the seller of the house to apply to the landlord, and buy the house only when you know that the freehold can be bought on reasonable terms. You may have to come in on the seller's expenses, but your risk is reduced. Check with the building society of your choice that it is prepared to lend money on 'a leasehold with the right to purchase the freehold reversion'.

A buyer who is in the happy position of not needing a mortgage can sometimes pick up a lease of medium length at a much lower price than a comparable freehold house, but let him beware of buying during the last ten years or so, without having a very thorough survey of the house. At the end of the lease he has to return the house to the ground landlord. Not only does he have to return it, but it must be in the condition stipulated by the lease, and that lease commonly makes the lessee of the house responsible for keeping it well repaired and decorated. A house which has been up for some eighty or ninety years does not usually meet that standard and at the end of the lease the lessee may have to pay compensation to the landlord. In short, at the beginning of a lease there is not much to choose between buying freehold or leasehold; towards the end of a lease the same premises may not be worth buying. The rent is low but the responsibilities are very high.

Part Possession

Buying a house with part possession, say of the ground floor, is quite different from buying a ground floor flat. Flats – old and new – are dealt with in Chapter 10.

Part possession of a house may give you the ground floor to live in, but will also give you a measure of responsibility for the rest of the house and its inhabitants. How much responsibility depends on what kind of agreement the other people in the house have with the present owner. Such an agreement can be written into a lease or tenancy agreement or can be by word of mouth. The Rent Acts may also influence the relationship between landlord and tenant.

If you are lucky, the upstairs tenant has a long lease with a full repairing liability. In other words, he would have to chip in massively when the house needs repairs. Unfortunately, you are not likely to be offered that house with part possession. Far more probably, the owner of the house would offer you a flat on a long lease because, curiously enough, he could expect a better price that way.

No, the chances are that 'part possession' involves either a flat or some rooms for you, and a flat or further rooms occupied by tenants. It may be very nice to move into a house without being alone. Or again, it may not. If you do not get on with the tenants, you may nevertheless have to put up with them. You may not be able to raise their rent, you may not even be able to count on getting their accommodation when the present tenant dies and you outlive him. It is vital – if you don't want to risk nasty surprises later on – to get advice from your solicitor immediately.

Advantages:	Price will be lower than for a flat of similar size
	Company in the house
	Tenant provides you with an income
	Some of the outgoings on the house can be set off before you pay tax on the rent you receive
Snags:	Tenant's rent may be controlled by law at a low figure
	Tenant may have the right to pass tenancy on to another member of the family
	Tenant's habits may not agree with yours
	You may have to pay for major repairs to tenant's accommodation
	You are not likely to get a building society mortgage
	You will have to pay income tax on your profit from letting.

Sitting Tenants

If you are the tenant of a house, or of a flat, the owner may be willing to sell the house to you at less than its normal price. The reason does not necessarily lie in the owner's great affection for you. A reasonably well-behaved tenant can, if he wishes, continue to live in the place almost indefinitely. The owner, therefore, cannot sell the house as easily or for such a good price as the owner of a house without tenants. His difficulty may help you.

If you are wise, you will talk to an estate agent or solicitor before you start negotiating with your landlord.

Local Authority Houses

After three years' occupation of council property, tenants can buy it if they wish. Before you do this, however, you would be wise to talk it over with your solicitors. For more details on the matter, see Chapter 11.

Somebody Else Wants Your Chosen House

Make up your mind how badly you want the house. If you wish to buy it, do not delay. The sooner your solicitors make contact with the present owner's solicitors, the better your chances. Owners are usually impressed by the fact that a potential buyer is prepared to go to the length of visiting a solicitor. They accept it as a token of the buyer's seriousness. The solicitors will also be able to work out what they and you can do to speed up the buying process.

Chapter 8

The Deposit

The word 'deposit' means different things to different people. Result: confusion. No one meaning is either right or wrong; this chapter explains how some of those concerned with deposits – house agents, building societies, house-buyers – think of them. Read this chapter to help you plan your house-buying, and do not conclude that because one man says you need a deposit of £x and another that you need only £y the second is necessarily offering you better terms. One estimate may well include something that another leaves out. What matters to you is: how much money of your own do you need to buy the house? Chapter 4, 'The Cost of Buying and Running a House', gave the answer.

The present chapter is intended to help you to know what the 'experts' are talking about, also whether and when to hand money over to them. The important thing about a deposit is that it should be paid to the right person at the right time.

Preliminary Deposit

When you first tell an estate agent that you want to buy the house which he has shown you, he will tactfully suggest that you should pay a deposit. Possibly the owner of the house, when you tell him the glad news that you want to buy, will himself mention the deposit. They both have the same thing in mind: there is many a slip between saying you will buy a house and actually buying it; how are they to know whether you mean business or whether you are giving voice to a pious hope? If you can be persuaded to put down money you are more likely to take this matter of house-buying seriously. They know, even if you do not at this point, that putting down a deposit does not bind you to go on with your purchase, but nevertheless . . .

It may be the other way round. You have fallen in love with a house and want to make sure of it. How better can you secure it than by putting down a deposit, reserving it to yourself?

Let us get this clear: both sides, buyer and seller, are bound only when they have exchanged contracts for the sale of the house (more about this on page 142). Paying a deposit does not reserve the house to the eager buyer, nor does it bring certainty to the anxious seller.

This does not mean that you should never pay a preliminary deposit but there are some guidelines which are worth following.

Very occasionally, a seller will reserve a house for a limited time on payment of a deposit. In such a case, check with a solicitor or some other reputable source that you are safe in paying.

Generally, a seller is more likely to put off other would-be buyers if he feels that you mean business. Some sellers are influenced by the fact that you have paid a deposit. Again, check before paying.

No one seriously expects you to pay more than a few hundred pounds at this stage; the cautious buyer leaves his cheque book at home and talks first to his solicitor. When the time comes, he pays the deposit through his solicitor, not direct to the seller.

If you pay a deposit to an estate agent, insist on a receipt and check its wording. Here is a typical receipt:

> Received from Mr Peter Piper the sum of £100 as preliminary deposit and in part payment of purchase money for the freehold property 14 Chestnut Avenue, Bursledon at the price of £   , subject to contract.
> Received the above sum as stakeholders.

Two phrases are important. First, 'stakeholders'; stakeholders are obliged to hold the deposit until completion of the sale; 'agents for the vendor' on the other hand are free to hand it over to the owner of the house. It is in your interest as buyer that the deposit money should remain where it is; if the sale is not completed you want your money back. The owner may need the deposit urgently and insist on it being paid to his solicitor as 'agent for the vendor'. The draft contract will make this clear. Your solicitor will warn you if your seller makes this condition. You are then in a dilemma: obviously, your deposit is safer if it cannot be touched by anyone. Against this, the vendor may not be able to sell to you unless he can use your deposit. Perhaps he needs it to pay a deposit on his new house, or perhaps he is a builder who has borrowed money to build your new home and who wants to reduce his bank overdraft as quickly as possible. Ask your solicitor to find out the reason why the seller wants to use your deposit; you can then assess with him how much of a risk you are taking. I sometimes try a compromise: half the deposit to be at the vendor's disposal, the other half to be kept by stakeholders until completion. Whatever you decide to do, at the early stage when an estate agent asks for a preliminary deposit, insist that he holds money you pay him 'as stakeholder'.

The words 'subject to contract' are even more important. They make it clear that you are not bound to buy the house till you exchange contracts. If for any reason, good or bad, you decide against signing a contract, you are entitled to claim your deposit back. This freedom is vital to you because at this stage you probably have no idea whether the house is soundly built (a survey will show), or whether you will be able to sell your own house in time, or whether you will be able to borrow enough money to buy. And it is always possible that one member of your family will take a dislike to the house, or that there are no suitable schools in the neighbourhood. It is true that, though you are not bound to go on, neither is the seller. He is free to accept another offer at any time until contracts have been exchanged. You cannot reasonably expect to bind one side without binding the other. Fortunately, sellers are usually prepared to wait if they feel that you are serious about their house.

Important
Do not pay a deposit to the house-owner direct or to a so-called 'conveyancing' firm.

Get a receipt.

See that the words 'as stakeholder' and 'subject to contract' are included in the receipt.

Do not sign anything till your solicitor tells you to.

New Houses

Houses on new estates are often sold direct by the company developing the estate and are not offered through estate agents. Some estate developers refuse to deal with you until you have paid a deposit and signed a lengthy document. Paying a deposit in such a case usually means that the house will be reserved for you at its present price – find out for how long – but almost inevitably the document will contain conditions for which you may not have bargained. One document I saw told the buyer that his £200 deposit would be used towards the purchase price if he exchanged contracts within six weeks. This sounds reasonable, but if he has read this book he will know the difficulty: once he signs on that particular dotted line he will have to buy that house or lose £200. In another case, the buyer was told nothing, not even shown building plans, until he had paid a non-returnable £50. Such a practice, though understandable from the developer's point of view, can add to the house-buyer's expenses. He may have to risk the loss of this non-returnable deposit or decide not to buy on that estate at all. If the house looks good, he usually decides to pay the deposit.

Dealing with the Owner

It is not only on a housing estate that you may deal direct with the owner. Perhaps you found the house not through an agent but through a newspaper advertisement put in by the owner, or through personal recommendation. It is all right for you to tell the owner that you like his house, that you hope to buy it, and to agree on a price. But do no more. Ask the name of his solicitor, and, if a deposit is wanted, pay his solicitor through your own solicitor (see Chapter 7).

Warning
Do not pay the owner, or you may have difficulty in getting your
deposit back if the sale does not go through.

10 Per Cent Deposit

A contract for the sale of a house almost invariably stipulates that
on exchange of contracts the buyer should pay 10 per cent of the
price; the remaining 90 per cent is paid on completion of the
purchase. The exchange of contracts, however, means more than
merely paying 10 per cent. The importance of exchanging contracts is that it marks the point of no return. Once you have
exchanged contracts with the seller, you *must* buy the house. If you
don't, you lose the deposit and you may even have to pay compensation to the seller if he then has to sell at a loss.

The 10 per cent deposit is not always paid at the moment when
contracts are exchanged. You may not have heeded my earlier
advice and have paid 10 per cent when you first decided on the
house. Or you may have paid a preliminary deposit when you first
decided to buy, and will bring the payment up to 10 per cent on
exchange of contracts. Your solicitor will tell you whether the
contract says you should pay the estate agent or the owner's
solicitor. Do not pay the owner direct. The best thing usually is to
leave your money invested till it is needed. If it is in a savings
account, or invested in securities, ask your solicitor to give you as
much warning as possible so that you can get the deposit ready.

A further point worth consideration: on a house costing, say,
£24,000, you are expected to pay a deposit of £2,400 about a
month before you can move in. £2,400 invested at 10 per cent
would bring in £20 during that month; £2,400 borrowed from a
bank will cost even more. When house prices and interest rates are
high, you might, therefore, try to persuade the owner to take a
deposit of less than 10 per cent. You might reasonably argue that
your deposit is meant to assure him that you will not break your
contract, and that if he holds, say, £1,000 of your money he is

sufficiently protected against your backing out. Or you might try to persuade the seller's solicitor to invest the deposit in a building society and to give you the interest. Either ploy is worth trying, but do not be disappointed if you are repulsed.

What if you have to sell your present house to raise the deposit on the new? Talk this over with your solicitor and with the manager of your bank. When you have a firm offer for your present house, the bank will probably lend you the 10 per cent without making too much difficulty (this is the famous 'bridging loan'). Of course, you will have to show that the sale of your present house will leave enough money over to repay the bank. The bank will probably also be willing to lend you money for the deposit for a few days while you sell securities or get money out of a deposit account. Obviously, you will save money if you can avoid borrowing.

If you are selling one house to buy another you could try to get the first deposit paid to your solicitor 'as agent for the vendor'. An 'agent for the vendor', unlike a stakeholder, can use the money for the purposes of his client. It could therefore be used to provide the deposit on your new house and you would not have to borrow from your bank. Unfortunately, this convenient arrangement gives the buyer less security if the seller defaults; your buyer may insist on his deposit being held by stakeholders. But there is no harm in trying: more and more deposits are being used in this way when interest rates are high.

95 Per Cent Mortgage

What if you have been promised a 95 per cent mortgage by a building society or a local authority? You have put by the remaining 5 per cent and enough to cover removal and legal fees, and worked out that you have just enough to cover all contingencies. Then all of a sudden you get a letter from your solicitor asking you for a 10 per cent deposit. Your first reaction may be that he has made a mistake and that he ought to have asked the building society for the money. But, unfortunately, he can't. The lender will not part with money before completion of the purchase. In the meantime contracts have to be exchanged or the sale will fall through.

There is usually a way out. You may be able to borrow part of the deposit, privately, or from your bank, on the strength of the 95 per cent mortgage offer. If all else fails, it is worth trying to see whether the owner will accept a deposit of only 5 per cent. Provided you can satisfy his solicitor that you really have an offer of a 95 per cent mortgage and that there are no other snags, you may find that this is the easiest way out. Tell your solicitor on your very first visit that you are counting on a mortgage of more than 90 per cent and will not be able to raise a 10 per cent deposit. This will avoid last minute panic.

Size of Deposit

The most important thing from your point of view is not so much *when* you pay a deposit as *how much* you have to pay in all. Many house-buyers sensibly concentrate on working out how much they will have to find out of their own pocket, and look on that sum as 'the deposit'. Many building societies do likewise. The building society, when you apply for a mortgage, always asks 'How much are you going to contribute?' The answer in short is: the difference between the mortgage and the purchase price. This is explained in detail on pages 59–60 (capital contribution). But do not forget all the other figures of Chapter 4. The 'deposit', however you define it, is not all you need. Make sure, before you get too deeply involved in house-buying, that you have enough money to pay the deposit when contracts are exchanged; enough to buy the house and to pay all the attendant fees when the purchase is being completed; and that you can spare enough from your income to pay the outgoings once you have bought the house.

Chapter 9

Surveyors

With your application for a mortgage you normally pay a fee, often called a 'survey fee', though not by a building society or local authority, who are more likely to refer to an 'inspection fee'. This is more than a matter of words: before it commits itself to lending money, the society gets a surveyor to inspect the house to make sure that it is worth lending on, i.e. that it is structurally sound and so forth.

Some building societies and most local authorities employ their own surveyors. Others instruct local surveyors to do the job. The thoroughness with which the inspection is made varies very much from one surveyor to another. Some inspect a house in great detail, others merely look at the outside, particularly if the house is in an area with which they are thoroughly familiar.

The surveyor makes a report to the building society and may include in it comments on the state of repair of the house and suggestions for work which should be done. On the basis of this report the society either offers the amount for which you have asked or a lesser amount, or refuses your application. Or again it may say: you can have the loan but we shall hold back part of it till you have done certain repairs. It gives you a list of repairs and usually sets a time limit.

A typical example was that of a friend of Jones. He was offered a mortgage subject to a retention by the society till he had re-pointed the west wall. He was allowed six months to do the job. He took the smaller sum, bought the house, and immediately got in a builder. As soon as the pointing was complete, he told his solicitor. The surveyor came back to make sure that the work had been properly done and reported to the building society, which then handed over the balance less a small fee for their surveyor.

Most building societies lend up to about 80 per cent of their surveyor's valuation on a modern house, less on a house built before 1918. This figure can often be increased by an insurance policy, guaranteeing another 10 or 15 per cent, thus giving you a mortgage of up to 95 per cent. But you should understand that this is 95 per cent of the building society's valuation, and not necessarily 95 per cent of the price you will have to pay for the house. You will be offered 95 per cent of the price only if in the surveyor's view the house is worth at least what you are paying for it. Building societies, however, always play safe and point out that an offer of £x does not mean that in their view the house is worth that sum. On the other hand, a refusal by a building society to lend money on a particular house should make you think again. If the society does not want to sink money into that house, do you really want to buy it? If the society offers less than you have asked for, try to find out the reason. If the reason is connected with their surveyor's valuation, again ask yourself whether you are paying more than the house is worth.

The building society's object in sending a surveyor is to make sure that next time the house is sold it is likely to fetch at least enough to repay the mortgage. The buyer wants to know much more. His concern is with the value, certainly, and he should if he has read the earlier chapters have a fair idea of values before he signs a contract. But it is even more important for him to know whether the house which he is about to buy has any defects not apparent on inspection, defects which may cost a lot to put right.

Some of the answers will be given, free of charge, by a firm of woodworm and dry rot specialists. There are many such firms. They give a report, an estimate of what it would cost to remedy the defect, and the promise of a guarantee for anything up to thirty years. It is worth remembering, though, that the firm does not guarantee to stay in business for thirty years. If you are looking for a mortgage on an old house, the building society or local authority may well make it a condition that you get such a report. Look carefully at the estimate: it will explain what is included and what is not. A damp house drying out, for example, will often need a great deal done to its plasterwork. Such work is not always included in the estimate.

Houses built within the last few years may carry a National House-Building Council certificate. This runs for a maximum of ten years and deals only with major defects. Neither an NHBC certificate nor a woodworm guarantee covers the full range of ills that can befall a house.

For this reason it is a good idea to have the house surveyed before you decide whether to buy. It would of course be simpler, and possibly cheaper, if the building society surveyor not only inspected the house for the society, but at the same time surveyed it for the purchaser. Indeed many people not surprisingly think that is what does happen. But they are wrong. The building society surveyor, as explained, makes a report to his client, the society, mainly on the value of the house. He does not make a survey of the structure, which is a much more detailed affair, nor does he owe any duty to the buyer of the house. He works for the society and looks after its interests. If he thinks the house is worth less than you are offering, he values it at a lower price but neither he nor the society necessarily tells you how much lower. If he makes a mistake, he is responsible only to the society, which may decide never to employ him again. But you are still left with your mortgage debt if you bought the house relying merely on the mortgage offer. One of the big societies has recently introduced the practice of at least showing the buyer the report it gets from its surveyor. Others may well follow suit.

Buyers, however, should not deceive themselves. Without a full surveyor's report, made on their own instructions, they have not given themselves every chance of finding out about the house while there is time to pull back.

A budget which does not allow for repairs might be seriously thrown out by the sudden emergence of fractured drains, dry rot in the floor or settlement in the main walls. It may take years for these faults to show, but when they do you may have to spend a lot of money. It is possible for woodworm to be present for many years without being detected. It is also possible that the owner knows there is woodworm but does not tell you. He does not have to volunteer information about the defects of his house. All he need do is give a straight answer to your questions. Not being a surveyor, you will find it difficult to know what questions to ask. Even if you put the right questions, it is open to the owner to say: 'Come and look for yourself.'

In spite of the expense you would, therefore, be wise to employ a surveyor of your own. You may know one. If not, try to get a recommendation. You want a surveyor who is thorough and who takes responsibility for his job. You do not want to spend money on a report like one I once saw, which excluded roof and floor boards and ended with a sentence to the effect that while every care had been taken no responsibility could be accepted for its contents. Many estate agents have at least one chartered surveyor in the partnership who can do the survey for you, but never employ a member of the firm of estate agents who are selling you the house: their duty to the owner may conflict with their duty to you. It would also be better not to employ an agent who is anxious to sell you a different house from the one he is being asked to survey. It is worth asking the building society whether they will give you the name of the surveyor who looks at the house for them. He may be willing to do a full survey for you while he is at the house.* This is usually a little cheaper, and means one visit fewer for the harassed owner of the house. Not every surveyor who does building society work also does full structural surveys. In some firms there are specialists for each job, emphasizing the fact that the two are by no means identical.

There is no set fee so it is advisable to agree on one before telling the surveyor to go ahead. Also tell him exactly what you want done; his fee will depend on his professional qualifications, the size, age and accessibility of the house and on what work you expect him to do. His ordinary fee may not include a test of the drains or of the electric wiring. If you want these checked, as you should in the case of an elderly house, tell him before he goes. He may be able to do the job himself, or to arrange for someone else to go with him.

A good surveyor will not only come back with a report of the

---

* Some building societies offer this option.

state of repair obvious to the observant layman – cracks, broken tiles, etc. – but he will also cast an expert eye on the less obvious places and tell you whether the roof is sound, whether he suspects settlement, dry rot, wet rot, woodworm, rising damp or any of the other ills which tend to befall houses. Do not be too shattered if your dreamhouse suffers from some of these. No house, it would seem, is completely free from defect. Furthermore, some go on happily in their defective state. The surveyor will tell you how serious the trouble is. If it can be put right, you can then ask a builder how much this would cost. You may well find that the owner is willing to pay part of the cost of remedying a defect; frequently a surveyor's report more than pays for itself. Of course, as well as a surveyor, you should get a specialist firm to check the house for woodworm, dry rot, rising damp, etc.

Some chartered surveyors are willing to do a limited report for potential house-buyers for a much lower fee. It leaves out a number of things a buyer is likely to want to know and is not really a substitute for a complete survey.

Chapter 10

Buying a Flat or a New House

Flats

Not everyone takes kindly to the thought of living in a flat. Some people think of the dreadful experience of those whose flats have exploded, or collapsed, who were stuck in lifts, or marooned on the fifteenth floor. People on the continent do not necessarily love their flats, but have apparently come to terms with them. I often visit a friend in Rome whose balcony is a bower of roses, whose children have grown up without noticeable signs of deprivation, who never has to mow the lawn or to worry about muddy boots on the carpet. The flat is on the second floor, the common staircase not only absorbs mud and dust, but also provides a place where neighbours can meet.

The price of land in England is high: modern builders therefore tend to put as many dwellings on each plot as possible. More and more flats are being built, particularly in large cities. More and more people are, therefore, now thinking about buying a flat, particularly for their first home. Flats fall, roughly, into three groups:

Conversions

A large family house, often Victorian – intended for a large Victorian family with its complement of many children, maiden aunts and servants – is cut up into several flats. In a building of three or four floors this may result in three or four, or six or eight, spacious and attractive self-contained units, each with its own access, kitchen, bathroom, etc. However, not every conversion is done with an eye to beauty and suitability. It could be a neglected house, divided into separate units by sheets of hardboard, with downpipes sprouting under the windows.

A converted flat can sometimes be found in a neighbourhood where there are few flats; it may have interesting proportions, and it may cost less than a purpose-built flat.

More and more first-time buyers look for conversions. They value the extra space, the funny corners, the low price. There are snags though: they may end up in draughty, high-ceilinged rooms, with a lot of noise from next door. The main disadvantage, particularly for first-time buyers, is that it may be difficult to get a mortgage. Also, some building societies charge slightly higher interest on converted flats.

Purpose-built Flats (originally intended for letting)

Such flats were often built in big cities in the years before 1939. By modern standards they tend to be spacious, are usually well constructed and in substantial buildings. Being built for letting, there is sometimes a supply of hot water, or central heating, from one central source. There may even be a communal restaurant, a lift, or a porter. Such flats are often modernized by the owner of the building as tenants move out, and then offered for sale. They are often less expensive than more recently built flats, and they are frequently far more solid. Against this, communal services may be more expensive than those you provide yourself: are you not more careful with hot water for which you receive a quarterly bill than with water from a boiler you have never seen?

Modern Flats (those built since about 1960)

Because of the high price of land and because the Rent Acts make being a landlord hazardous and unprofitable, almost all privately built flats are put up with a view to sale. Each flat is usually provided with its own front door as well as its own means of heating.

The advantages of such a flat are usually most obvious to young couples, though older couples whose children have grown up and moved away may find them equally useful. The majority of these flats have one or two bedrooms and one living room. The kitchen is usually equipped with built-in cupboards. Sometimes there are also built-in wardrobes, woodblock flooring or other luxuries. There is no difficulty about getting a maximum mortgage. Very little furniture is needed to make a flat into a home. The price both of buying and of maintaining a modern flat is probably lower than that of a house.

The snags? The rooms in such flats tend to be small, with little space for large pieces of furniture or for the accumulated junk of a happy family. The flat may or may not provide a reasonable standard of sound-proofing; you live at close quarters with your neighbours and cannot afford to fall out with them. In some London suburbs so many flats are being built that it may become more difficult to sell them. The rateable value of a flat tends to be comparatively higher than of a house; the cost of maintenance cannot be controlled by you (more about this later in this chapter) whereas in your own house you can decide not to paint this year because of unexpected roof repairs.

Very important

Make sure the lease of the flat you intend to buy has a good number of years left. A new or newly converted flat will probably offer a lease of at least ninety years. You may think thirty or forty quite long enough for your needs, but it is not: you will be putting down several thousand pounds to buy that lease and you will probably want to sell it again. A lease with under forty-five or fifty years to run will be hard to sell. Nor is anyone likely to grant a mortgage on it. The chief worry of every building society, or of any lender for that matter, is that the building must at least keep its value till the mortgage is repaid. To be on the safe side, try for a flat where the lease will go on for a minimum of another seventy years.

Let us follow Jack String on his hunt for a flat. Life in a flat comes naturally to him: his mother has lived in one since she was widowed many years ago. Jack remembers the joy of racing up to the sixth floor while a more sedate adult made his ponderous way up by lift. His mother's flat is on the top floor of a block of flats built in about 1925. The flat used to have a view over the river, and now has a view over chimneys and TV aerials. She chose a top floor because she loves Italian opera which she plays loudly at all hours. The block of flats, being somewhat old-fashioned, has only two flats on each floor, divided by a stairwell. Very little sound, therefore, travels from her flat to her neighbours'. There is a resident porter who admits callers only after checking with the owner of the flat and there has never been a burglary. He also operates the lift and, if asked nicely, unstops the sink and mends fuses for Jack's mother.

Jack is in the pleasant stage between bachelordom and marriage, and his girlfriend will probably come to share the flat; they have little furniture between them. They have looked at a flat rather like his mother's but decided against it because the central-heating system serving the block was some forty years old and likely to need replacing before long. Jack did not want to be saddled with a major expense of this kind. Nor can he easily afford the porter's wages or the upkeep of the thick carpets on the stairs.

Jack works in the West End of London. He has come to the view that whereas the choice in his favourite area, Kensington, is very restricted at a price he can afford, there seem to be very many flats to be had further out. After receiving a list of some fifty flats from one agent and inspecting several of these, he decides to make a detailed list of his requirements:

Must have	*Would like*
Price below £x thousand	Price about £x thousand
Near public transport	Separate WC
Three rooms	Garden
Full central heating	Fitted carpets
	Double glazing
	East/west aspect
	Balcony

Jack's girlfriend has ideas of her own. She does not make a list but makes a mental note to look out for a flat with a balcony and with space for a pushbike or a pram either in the flat or elsewhere in the building.

Eventually Jack visits Dragon Court. On either side of the entrance of a stark modern building there are two heraldic beasts justifying the name of the Court. The entrance hall is carpeted; he cannot hear himself walk. The staircase is covered in vinyl which is slightly noisy but means that the stairs will not need recarpeting every few years. The sound of shuffling footsteps is a good deal less obtrusive than on the concrete stairs Jack has climbed in some of the other blocks he has looked at. Jack is impressed. The flat itself has a small lobby with doors to all rooms, another good point in his eyes. In several other flats one had to go through the lounge to reach the bathroom and bedrooms. This might suit a young family, but does not allow for grown-ups who want to get in and out without disturbing one another.

There is full central heating – another plus point; some flats have central heating in only two rooms; in others the water has to be heated separately by gas or electricity. Jack likes a warm bathroom and plenty of hot water at reasonable cost. Bathroom and WC are combined; indeed Jack has seen no modern flat at a price he could contemplate which afforded the luxury of a separate lavatory.

The bedrooms face east, the lounge west, ideal for a sun-worshipper who is out during the day: he would wake up to sunlight and be home again to enjoy the evening sun. The view from the living room is on to a paved area, interrupted only by standard roses and ornamental trees – pleasant to look at and simple to maintain.

The owner tells Jack that he intends to leave behind the fitted carpets in two rooms. Jack makes a note to check with his solicitor – he has decided that this is the flat for him – whether the lease requires him to carpet the flat throughout.

In some of the very new flats which Jack has seen the rooms were so tiny that they would hardly hold his small store of furniture. This flat is some fifteen years old and not quite so tightly planned. Jack also remembers what a surveyor friend has told him: a building needs a few years to show whether it is going to have problems. After ten or twelve years one can tell whether cracks are serious or not.

Next day Jack telephones the estate agent and makes an offer,

£300 below the asking price. After looking at the list of flats it seems to Jack that he has a reasonable chance of getting this reduction. The agent telephones back within the hour: the owner will take a reduction of £200. Jack accepts gracefully and tells the agent to go ahead. He gives him the name and address of his own solicitors. Jack then rings his solicitors and tells them of the intended purchase. He also makes an appointment with them a fortnight ahead. By then the solicitors ought to have received a copy of the lease from the owner's solicitors, and should be able to tell Jack about its good and bad points.

Next, Jack goes to the building society with whom he wisely put his savings some years earlier. The manager of the building society has already told Jack that he can have the money he needs, provided the flat passes muster. When Jack visits his solicitors they go through the lease together. Practically all flats in England (not so in Scotland) are offered for sale on long leases (leasehold). The general rule that freehold has the edge on leasehold does not apply to flats, or to maisonettes. There are reasons, buried in legal history, which make it difficult for one freehold-owner to force another to look after his flat. And if the people above and below you will not look after the paintwork of their flats, your own flat will probably lose value. Worse still, if the gutter on the top floor is allowed to leak, the people on all floors below may suffer from damp walls. Other things being equal, try to buy a flat leasehold. In an old flat it can nevertheless happen that no one is responsible for upkeep of the building. Modern flats are usually well organized in this respect.

Often the land and those parts of the building not forming part of any flat (the common parts) are either left in the hands of the builder, or sold to a management company in which each flat-owner has a share. From the flat-owner's point of view, a management company is probably the most labour-saving way of having the block well maintained. The company works on a business footing and charges for the work it does. The charges are fairly strictly controlled by law. Before the company orders expensive work, the flat-owners must be consulted and several estimates obtained. The flat-owners themselves sometimes feel that they could arrange the work more cheaply. Residents who are prepared to spend time on this can ask different firms for estimates, do some of the work themselves and get to know one another as well as save money. In my experience flat-owners can be rallied when there is a crisis (e.g. a very large bill), but they are unlikely to take a continued interest in running a block.

At Dragon Court the running of the block is in the hands of a firm of estate agents. Jack was concerned that this might be very expensive, but is reassured when the present owner tells him that he has had to pay only a few pounds a week, including insurance of the flat.

Dragon Court follows a fairly common pattern. The block of flats stands back from the road; there is a separate block of garages, and a place where all the dustbins are kept. All flats are reached through the same front door, entrance hall and staircase.

When the flats were built, the builder granted a 99-year lease for each flat. Each lease contains a clause saying that there is a yearly rent of £20 for each of the first 30 years, after which the rent goes up to £50 a year. That rent (the 'ground rent') is paid by the owner of the flat to the owner of the land. His lease gives the flat-owner the right to use the communal parts he needs: a right to walk from the street to his own front door; from his flat to the dustbin and to the garden, a right to use the garden and a right to drive his car to his garage.

He also gets the right to enter an adjoining flat in an emergency, and similarly he must allow his neighbours to come into his flat if, for instance, there is a gas leak, or water coming through the ceiling. He will have to keep his flat in good repair – the lease says what bits are his and what bits will be done communally. At Dragon Court each flat-owner looks after the interior and the landowner looks after the outside. The lease obliges each flat-owner to contribute to the cost of the communal work, and to the cost of insuring the block against fire, etc. The landowner in his turn promises to repair and insure the building and to look after the common parts.

During the fortnight before he went to see his solicitors, Jack thought of a number of points. He now tries to get them clarified:

(1) Will he need carpets throughout the flat? If everyone has to carpet throughout, the flats will be quiet but the expense considerable.

(2) Will he have to pay stamp duty on the rent? No, because this is not a new lease. When the lease was granted to the first flat-owner, it was stamped. The stamped lease will form part of Jack's title deeds. Jack himself is liable for stamp duty only on the price he pays for the flat. The agreed price £30,100 includes fitted carpets. Jack pays for these separately and saves. Houses and flats attract stamp duty, carpets don't. By buying the latter separately, it may be possible to pay less stamp duty, or none at all. A flat bought for £30,100 including £500 worth of carpets attracts stamp duty at 1 per cent, i.e. £301. However, there is no stamp duty on a flat bought for £29,600 (being below the £30,000 threshold for stamp duty), nor on carpets, however expensive. Jack can therefore save £301 by telling his solicitor that he is buying the owner's carpets.

(3) Does he repair the outside of his flat? No, but he has to pay a proportion of the cost of maintaining Dragon Court in good order. This point is particularly important for the buyer of a top floor flat. If he is solely responsible for his flat (including the roof) he must have the roof carefully surveyed: roof repairs are very expensive.

(4) Are there any major outstanding repairs? The answer will probably have to be given by a surveyor – see Chapter 9.

(5) How easy is access to all parts of the building which may need repair or maintenance? If the window cleaner needs a cradle he will charge more than if he can reach all windows with ease. If the back of the house can be reached only over the roof or through your flat, repairs could be both expensive and inconvenient. (Victorian conversions and flats over shops are particularly apt to have this problem.)

A modern flat is as popular with most building societies as a modern house. You will be able to borrow the same high percentage on either. Just occasionally one society's rules work against a particular type of lease. You are unlikely to change the provisions of the lease, so go to another building society. If you are buying a flat in a brand-new development, the developer may have made arrangements with a particular building society. Ask about this – you are not obliged to use that society but it may save time and trouble to try them first of all.

New Houses

Similar rules apply to new houses – building societies are glad to lend. Provided your income is, in their eyes, large enough for the mortgage, you can probably borrow 90 to 95 per cent of their valuation.

If the house is completely built when you decide to buy, no special precautions are necessary, except to ask whether it carries a National House-Building Council certificate. Buying a house without NHBC insurance could lead to a problem when reselling, at least within the ten years' protection provided by the certificate.

It helps to buy on an estate where you can see at least one completed show house. Try to disregard its tasteful furnishing and find out what will come with your house and what has to be paid for separately. In times of sluggish sales there may be extras included in the price to induce you to buy. A very helpful incentive of this sort is aid with the mortgage in case of redundancy.

When there are more buyers than houses, every house on an estate may well be sold before the first one has been built. At such times you may see some rather elegant pictures and be told that the house will have woodblock flooring in the sitting-room, or a coloured bathroom suite. Many new houses have one touch of luxury of this kind and very nice it is too, but do not be dazzled by the glamour of a fitted kitchen; what you really need is a solidly built house whose walls and roof will stand up to time. If the building gives little trouble, you will be able to afford a beautiful interior; you will, on the other hand, get little comfort when the wind blows through cracks in the walls of your super American ranch-style lounge.

Check on how the house will be heated, whether central heating extends to all rooms and whether there is double glazing. Compare the room measurements given with the size and proportion of actual rooms. The building specification itself is something on which you would do well to get a surveyor's opinion. Be very suspicious of a builder who refuses to disclose plans and specifications before you have signed a binding contract.

Again, make sure the house will have an NHBC insurance cover. It is given only to builders who agree to build to the standards laid down by the National House-Building Council. The Council inspects the house periodically during construction. The builder guarantees that the house is constructed according to the Council's standards (or to the conditions laid down in the building contract where these are higher) and that it will be built in a workmanlike manner and be fit for human habitation.

The builder agrees to make good any defects appearing within two years because of a breach of these standards – other than cracks, etc. caused during the drying-out process. Central heating is covered for one year only.

If the builder should go out of business during the guarantee period, the Council steps into his place.

For a further eight years the Council itself undertakes to make good major defects, such as a collapsing roof, or severe damage caused by subsidence. The maximum insurance cover goes up each year in step with inflation.

It is a useful guarantee and the majority of reputable builders are content to give it. Even if you yourself would be prepared to do without, you should spare a thought for the future when you may want to sell the house. Building societies are becoming increasingly reluctant to lend money on houses without the NHBC insurance: more about this in the booklet *Your New House*, prepared by the National House-Building Council.

Stage Payments

All the houses so far mentioned have to be paid for in the same way: 10 per cent on exchange of contracts and the balance on completion.

Some new houses, particularly those put up by small firms, are paid for in a different way: by stage payments. The contract provides for a down payment and for further instalments when the building is up to the first floor, up to roof level, ready for plastering, etc. As each stage is reached, the builder collects an instalment. Building societies, if they are willing to lend at all on the house, can usually be persuaded to provide money as each stage is reached, though not until their surveyor has had a look at the construction and declared himself satisfied. He charges a small fee for each inspection. Also, each instalment paid out by the building society bears interest as soon as it is handed over. Stage payments benefit the builder rather more than the house-buyer, who has to make mortgage payments *before* he has a house to move to. Some builders, recognizing the buyer's problem, offer him a rented house while his new one is being built. This makes it possible for him to sell his old home, invest the money and pay it out to the builder as each stage is reached.

Buying a Plot

You may be in luck if you are offered a plot of land. Make sure that it has planning permission for the kind of building you would like to put on it. Outline permission for one private house is likely to allow just that; don't count on putting up two and a chicken farm. Ready-made designs for houses can be bought for less than an architect's fee; they do, however, have a way of not fitting your plot. You need imagination as well as a reliable builder.

If the plot is in the country, do not forget the dull details – how far must electricity be brought, how will the property be drained, has the plot access to a road, etc.?

You may well get a much better, though certainly a more expensive, house if you have it specially designed for your plot and your needs.

Chapter 11

Other Possibilities

Buying an Old House

Perhaps you are thinking of buying an old house because of its mellowness, its beautiful proportions, its Adam fireplace. A house of that kind needs a constant supply of money and love, and it is as well to remember that when you run out of one or both you cannot jettison your erstwhile love without finding a successor. You will probably take the advice of a surveyor or an architect before deciding on the purchase.

At the other end of the financial scale, you may well be thinking of an old house, not because it is beautiful but because it costs less than a more modern one. 'Old' in this context is not so much a matter of years as of lack of amenities. From time to time there are houses on the market without such aids to gracious living as a bathroom or a WC. They are well worth considering, provided they are structurally sound – and provided you can persuade a building society or local authority to lend you money. The absence of modern amenities can be an advantage, because you will almost certainly be able to claim a grant from the local authority to help provide them. How much you can hope to get depends on where you live and what improvements you want to make. In an area where there is a serious housing problem the council can give you a higher proportion of your expenses (up to 75 per cent) than in an ordinary one (up to 50 per cent). In an ordinary area you can get:

Bath/shower	£285
Water to bath	£360
Basin	£110

Water to basin	£190
Sink	£285
Water to sink	£240
WC	£430

Be careful though: these are the top figures, calculated to represent one half of the cost of modernization. If you do the work yourself, at less than twice the scale figure, your grant is reduced.

There are also further discretionary grants, subject to different rules, and hedged with exceptions. Do not rely on a grant but get a copy of the booklet *Your Guide to House Renovation Grants* from your local council.

The council normally expects you to apply for a grant before you start the work for which you want it. It is as well to go one further, and to find out the exact conditions on which a grant will be made before deciding whether you can afford to buy that house.

Homesteading

In some areas where there are many elderly houses in need of restoration, local authorities buy them up and resell them to first-time buyers at reasonably favourable prices. If you are a good handyman, find out whether your council runs the Homesteading Scheme and get particulars from them.

The houses are sold subject to a condition that you carry out specified repairs. The usual grants are available and the council keeps a close eye on your progress, setting a time limit for completing work. The advantage is that you don't have to start making mortgage payments until this limit is reached.

Buying a Thatched Cottage

A thatched cottage, if well looked after, should be acceptable to most building societies. Insurance rates will be higher than for a tiled or slated roof: the Country Gentlemen's Association may be able to make recommendations.

Buying by Auction

The 'Property for Sale' columns in newspapers, and advertisements in London underground stations, often offer houses for sale by auction. As a general rule these are either houses for investment, sold with a 'sitting tenant', or one-off houses for which it is not easy to fix a market price. A house resembling all the others in the road and offered with vacant possession is far more likely to be sold by private treaty.

Let us assume you are attracted to a house offered by auction. First see the agent and try to find out what sort of price the owner expects, or hopes for. If the agent won't tell you, put in an offer and see whether the owner is prepared to sell before auction at your figure. The great majority of houses offered for auction are sold long before. If your offer is not accepted and you are still keen on the house you must inevitably spend money before you know whether you are going to be successful at the auction, because the acceptance of your bid means that you have to sign a binding contract immediately after the auction. By that time, therefore, you must be sure that you will be able to raise the money, are satisfied about the soundness of its construction, and have explored its future with the local authority. Get advice on this from a solicitor well before the auction.

Buying by Tender

Occasionally a house is bought in this manner: you are asked to make an offer. If this is accepted you must buy. Make sure you have made all the inquiries recommended for auction sale *and* have taken advice on what is a reasonable price. Not a method to be advised.

Buying a Local Authority House

Council tenants of at least three years' standing can buy their houses or flats if they wish. The price is at least one third less than market value; the longer you have been a tenant the greater your discount.

If you are interested in buying and think that you qualify, fill in an application form. The council will in due course give you a price and will also make a mortgage offer of two and a half times the main income plus (in the case of joint buyers) once the second income; maximum 100 per cent of the price.

Advantages:
: Price likely to be considerably lower than comparable house bought on the open market

: Price frozen as soon as application to buy has been made (however long it takes the council to complete its paperwork)

: Tenant has right to freeze price for two years by paying £100 deposit, if mortgage offered by council is too low for his needs

Snags:
: The building may be in a poor state of repair and may need decorating

: There may be ground rent or a service charge to pay – ask the council about this before you buy

: Future repairs and maintenance will be your responsibility

: The 'market value' on which you get a discount is not necessarily the price at which you will be able to resell the house

: If you resell within five years you have to repay part of the discount

Consider:
: Is the house/flat in reasonable repair?

: If not, how much will it cost to put into an acceptable state? Can you increase your mortgage to pay for repairs/improvements?

How does your rent compare with the mortgage, rates and heating you will have to pay after you have bought?

Allowing for this extra expense, is it still a bargain?

Buying from Executors

It may well be of no interest or significance that a house is being sold by executors. When you buy a house through an advertisement or an estate agent you may not even be told that it is the late owner's executor who is selling. Some executors fear the knowledge of a recent death in a house may detract from its saleability.

It does not follow that executors will sell more cheaply than other owners. Occasionally, however, you can pick up a house, perhaps a little old-fashioned, not too recently painted or papered, at a lower price, simply because the executor lives a long way off and does not want the responsibility of maintenance. Or, the proceeds of sale may have to be shared by several people: a reduction, sizeable to you, may only mean a couple of hundred pounds less for each of them. There are several other reasons why an executor's sale may mean a bargain. Don't rely on this, but keep your eyes open for the possibility.

Housing Associations

If you have spent the past few years sharing a flat, your main idea in buying a house may well be to gain a little privacy. You may not warm to the idea of further communal effort. On the other hand, you will have learnt that by pooling your resources with others, you live much better than you could have done on your own.

Most housing associations exist to make rented homes available, but there are possibilities for those who want to own.

The types of association most likely to be of use to the would-be house-owner are either a *co-ownership association* or a *self-build association*. A recent development is *shared ownership* schemes.

Co-ownership Association

Co-ownership does not mean that you share your house; it means that the association owns a development, and you own shares in the association together with the right to occupy a particular property. You do not own that particular house or flat. This may not matter to you while you live there. Your 'rent' is likely to be lower than normal *and* it qualifies for mortgage interest relief.

What happens when you wish to leave? Not being an 'owner' you cannot sell your house, or your lease. But you can sell your share in the association. The rules of the association will lay down how much you can expect. Very roughly, this will be what you have put in, plus, if you have lived there for a number of years, a share in the increased value of the association property, less any outstanding liabilities. Obviously, if you leave after a short time you will get little or nothing, but the same may well be true of a house which you bought on mortgage. In the long run your profit on leaving tends to be lower than on a privately owned house.

Self-build Society

An excellent alternative to buying a house for those with (1) skills useful to housebuilding (e.g. architect, surveyor, bricklayer, plasterer) and (2) perseverance. A group of people combine to build a number of houses, all members of the group giving their services free. The cost of materials is provided by a local authority or building society mortgage with perhaps some contribution from members. As each house is completed it is made available to one of the members on loan, without protection from the Rent Acts. When all houses are finished each member can buy a house at a price which covers only the land, the building expenses and the mortgage. Each member then gets a mortgage of his own and becomes independent.

Shared Ownership

Some housing associations build blocks of flats for this purpose. Instead of buying the whole flat you buy a share in that flat and you rent the remainder. Although your purchase deed will put it in percentage terms, you buy – as it were – the living room and you pay rent for the rest. When you can afford some more, you buy the kitchen and pay rent only on the bedroom and bathroom, and so on, until you have either bought the whole flat or you want to sell.

This scheme may help you to find a roof over your head at a time when you cannot really afford to buy, but it is not a cheap method of buying. You buy your first slice today at today's value; by the time you buy your next slice, the value of the flat (and therefore the price of that slice) will have gone up.

Advice on all these schemes is obtainable from the Housing Corporation, Maple House, 149 Tottenham Court Road, London W1. To summarize:

Co-ownership:
Advantages:	Low capital contribution, favourable mortgage terms
Snags:	Difficult to find
	Even more difficult to form a new association
	Mortgage funds not always available
	Takes a long time.

Self-build:
The same advantages and disadvantages, plus
Advantages:	Standard of workmanship will probably be very high
	Low cost
Snag:	Special skills required.

Shared ownership:
Advantage:	You can buy in stages as your means allow
Snags:	You may not find a housing association with shared ownership flats in the area you want
	Later slices are likely to cost more than the first one
	You get tax relief only on your mortgage payment, not on your rent.

Part 3

Why It Takes So Long

Chapter 12

Solicitors' Work Before Contract

It is vital, if you want to buy a house as quickly as possible, to go to a solicitor as soon as you and the owner have agreed on a price and before you have committed yourself. Nevertheless, quite often a solicitor knows nothing of his client's intention to buy a house until he gets a letter from an estate agent, like the following:

Dear Sir,

re: 14 Chestnut Avenue, Bursledon

Acting on the instructions of Mr George Smith, we have sold the above property to Mr Peter Piper for £   . We understand that you act for Mr Piper. The vendor's solicitors are Messrs Blower & Co. of 8 High Street, Southampton, whom we have asked to send you a draft contract.

In the meantime, Mr Piper has paid us a preliminary deposit of £100. We enclose a copy of our receipt.

Yours faithfully,

Although agents often say they 'have sold' a house, in fact they have not at this stage. What they mean is that they are hoping to sell. The phrase, though often used by estate agents, does not bind you to go on with the purchase. Not, that is, unless you have disregarded the advice given in earlier chapters. Provided you have written no imprudent letters and signed no papers, you are not at this stage bound to buy. Equally, George Smith can change his mind about selling.

If the solicitor has not heard from Peter Piper before, he writes to him now for confirmation. Peter might reply:

Dear Mr Stokes,

Thank you for your letter. Yes, I am hoping to buy 14 Chestnut Avenue, Bursledon. The price is £   . I have applied for a mortgage of £   . I shall write to you again as soon as I know whether I can get enough money.

                    Yours sincerely.
                              Peter Piper

This tells the solicitor that Peter Piper is uncertain whether he will get his mortgage and does not want to incur solicitors' fees till he knows.

However, if he is in a hurry or is willing to risk a few pounds' extra expense, Piper will write a slightly different letter:

Dear Mr Stokes,

Thank you for your letter. Yes, I am hoping to buy 14 Chestnut Avenue, Bursledon. The price is £   . I have paid the agents £100 and have applied to the   Building Society, from whom you should be hearing shortly. Please in the meantime do what you can to speed up the purchase. I would like to move in seven weeks' time if possible.

                    Yours sincerely,
                              Peter Piper

This gives the solicitor the green light; it also tells him that everything will have to go according to programme, or seven weeks will not be long enough to see the purchase through.

He writes to the vendor's solicitors, Blower & Co., and asks for a draft contract. He may get it by return of post, or he may have to wait while the owner's solicitors track down the title deeds. To draft a contract a solicitor has to know what is in the title deeds. A prudent house-owner tells his solicitor as soon as he decides to sell his house. By the time he has found a buyer the solicitor will have either the deeds or a copy. Sometimes this is quite simple: some owners keep the deeds at home, some in their bank, and can send them to their solicitor. But when there is a mortgage on the house, there may be delay. The title deeds are with the lender – the bank, building society or insurance company. Some societies keep all deeds at their head office, others at different branches.

In the meantime, the buyer's solicitors will try to see their client and get all the information they need to do the job. Here is a list of questions to which sooner or later your solicitor will need the answers. It helps to have them ready for your first visit:

your full name and present address – for the purchase deed;

your occupation;

address of the new house;

present owner's name;

price;

freehold or leasehold;

whether you are buying through an agent. If so, his name and address;

whether you have paid a deposit and how much;

whether you need a mortgage and whether you have already applied for one (see below);

when you would like to move (see over);

whether you have to sell a house before you can buy this one;

whether you are buying any furniture with the house;

any fixtures;

whether you are buying in your sole name or with somebody else (see over);

most important: how definite are you about this house? When do you want the solicitors to start seriously on the legal work? As soon as you give your solicitors the go-ahead, they will make local authority searches and send out inquiries before contract (see p. 136–9).

Mortgage

If you have not yet applied for a mortgage your solicitors will be able to advise you. If the bulk of the purchase money is to be raised on mortgage, they will probably suggest that you visit a building society before you go further with your plans. Don't spend more on solicitors' fees till you know you can get a mortgage which is big enough to allow you to buy the house of your choice. What you *can* do is ask your solicitors to get a draft contract from the owner's solicitor. Once that has been sent out you will almost certainly be warned before the owner deals seriously with any other buyer. This is probably the nearest you can get to an assurance that the house will not be sold to anyone else.

Moving Date

Remember that the date you exchange contracts is not the date you move house. It is probably too early to fix a moving date, though it is convenient to plan about two months ahead – four weeks till contracts are signed, another four before moving. Do not make rigid plans, because you cannot rely on a date till you have exchanged contracts. There is a lot to do before you reach that stage. In particular, do not buy curtains or anything which might not fit equally well into another house should this deal fall through.

If this is the first house you are buying you may have to give your present landlord at least four weeks' notice. Tell your solicitors about this and they will arrange for you to know a month before you move. As soon as contracts are exchanged get in touch with removal firms, particularly if your move is planned for a weekend, a quarter day or near the end of the month – times at which they get most heavily booked.

The usual thing is to pay over your purchase money for the key of the house. Solicitors and agents talk of the 'completion date' – the day on which your purchase is finally tied up. Some owners allow the buyer to move in before completion, charging him rent in the meantime, but most prefer a straight exchange of money against key.

One Name or Joint Names?

In some homes the husband signs documents and later possibly tells his wife. In others nothing is decided till husband and wife have discussed it. This may determine whether the family home is bought in his name alone or in both names. Many couples feel that both husband and wife work to keep the house going and that they want to share in the ownership, so they buy the house in joint names.

A wife, particularly if she puts money into a house for the family, will probably feel more secure if her name is on the title deeds. She can be protected by law even if it is not, but anyone whose marriage is somewhat shaky would do well to talk to a solicitor at this stage.

Normally, when husband and wife buy in joint names, they do this with the idea that when one of them dies the other will automatically have the house. In law this is buying as 'joint tenants'. Some couples (or other joint buyers) prefer an arrangement whereby each can leave his/her share in the house to somebody else. This is buying as 'tenants in common', and is what the couple in the Land Certificate on pages 147–9 have done. The reason might be that a third party, perhaps Mary Bennett's parents, has lent one of them money informally and the borrower wants to repay it on sale or death; or there could be tax reasons – a couple may well save Capital Transfer Tax by giving a share in the house to their children rather than to each other; or one of them may have children from an earlier marriage and wish them to have a share in the house. Another advantage of buying as tenants in common is that the joint owners can own the house in unequal shares. If, for example, Jack and Libby had decided to buy a house together, her contribution would have been bigger than his, because she came out of her divorce with a capital sum. They might have decided that she should own a bigger share in the house.

Selling One House and Buying Another

When you sell one house and buy another you will probably need the money from your present house to pay for the new. Your buyer won't hand over his money except against your key, and you can't give up your old house except to move into the new. So both sales have to be completed on the same day. This can be a matter of considerable anxiety to you *and* to your solicitor: if anyone along the line is not ready in time, the whole transaction totters. When finance is fairly easy, a bank will often lend money for the new house pending the sale of the old – this is called a bridging loan.

Bridging Loan

Banks prefer to lend money for a short and definite period: ideally they want to be assured that you have a firm buyer for your old house and have exchanged contracts with him. This usually has to be confirmed by your solicitor direct to the bank.

A word of warning: bank loans are expensive. You have to pay interest, and in addition usually a fee for the work involved. Also, whenever government policy is against lending money, bridging loans are early victims. The solicitor can advise you on whether you are likely to have difficulty with your moving date, and what chance you have of a bridging loan. See your bank manager if you are likely to need a loan.

Local Authority Searches

Whenever they are concerned with buying a house, solicitors send a great number of questions to the local authority. They do not have a free hand in asking; they cannot ask how much the mayor paid for his own house, or whether the road is noisy. Questions have to be selected from about sixty agreed between the local authorities and the Law Society. The solicitors pay a fee, also agreed.

What happens when the questions reach the local authority? In a typical London borough all questions go to the Land Charges Department, which then collects the answers from other departments. For example, the GLC will be asked whether it has plans for road widening or compulsory purchase, the Public Health Department about smoke control or drainage, and the Borough Engineer whether the road is maintained at public expense. Eventually the questionnaire is returned to the solicitors with answers to all questions. How long it takes for a local authority to provide them varies considerably. Some local authorities send the answers back within a week, others take three or four weeks. Where a house lies in the area of an authority that takes a long time, a solicitor may advise that the inquiries should be put in even before you are quite sure that you will go through with the buying of the house. Local authorities' charges are £12·30. There is talk of local authorities being forced by law to reply in fourteen days, but there is no such law in force at the moment (autumn 1984). There is also talk of the information being made available, instantly, by computer. This project is not far beyond the pipedream stage.

The solicitors go through the answers and tell the buyer of any that may particularly affect him. For example, if the council plans to take over the private road outside the house, the owner of each house affected would have to contribute to the expense of making up the road. This could in effect add a few hundred pounds to the price of the house. If the council has got to the stage of knowing how much it will charge each frontager, it may be possible to get this contribution from the present owner. If the plan is at an early stage, the council may not know how much the work will cost. The buyer's solicitors will at least be able to warn their client.

Then there is smoke control. If a Smoke Control Order is to come into force in the near future, the house-owner will get a contribution from the local authority to convert open fires. A buyer can be warned not to lay in large supplies of fuel which he will not be able to use.

It is vital for every newly built house to fit in with the plans approved by the local authority. A buyer has to be sure, for example, that the house is not nearer the road than the authorized building line – it may have to be torn down if it offends. Or, again, there may be plans for road widening which might affect either house or garden. Or the drains, if private, might be taken over by the local authority – at the owner's expense. This can be required if there is a public sewer within 100 yards of the house. The search form will show whether there is.

As solicitors' questions have to follow a set formula, it is a good idea for you to visit the local town hall or council office yourself and to ask about future plans for the neighbourhood. These will only show on the 'local authority searches' if they are well advanced and if they directly affect your particular house. But there may be a vague proposal for a ring road within a few hundred yards of your house. You might want to know of any such plans, however vague, so that you can make up your minde whether they could put you off buying the house.

Inquiries Before Contract

Local authorities supply a great deal of information, yet this is not all a buyer needs to know. When his solicitors get the draft contract they will ask further questions of the present owner and his solicitors. This is usually done on a printed form containing some forty standard questions (not all of them have to be asked about each house). Useful information is provided about the existence of such things as rights of way, woodworm guarantees and fences. In addition, solicitors can ask other relevant questions. For a new house one would ask for a copy of any special conditions the council made when it gave permission to build; or it might be necessary to know whether a garage was put up in recent times. Many solicitors inquire about disputes with neighbours: a buyer might prefer to be warned before he walks into a quarrel over fences or rights of way. Local authorities as well as owners and their solicitors have to answer each question truthfully, but they do not have to volunteer information. Hence the need for so many questions.

Even so, there are a number of things about which you will not normally know before you exchange contracts. Your solicitors may ask whether there are disputes relating to the house but they cannot ask (and if they did the vendor could refuse to answer) what sort of people the neighbours are, whether quiet, fussy, noisy, or given to hysteria. Only time will tell. Nor will you know how much the vendor himself paid for the house. You can get some idea of whether you are paying the right price by comparing this house with others offered for sale in the area, and by asking a surveyor to give you his opinion. Comparing with other houses offered in the area is the cheaper method, but do not compare with similar houses elsewhere. Prices vary mysteriously from district to district, sometimes from road to road.

The Contract

When all questions have been asked and answered satisfactorily, the next step is the signing and exchange of contracts.

A contract is one of two vital documents required in the buying of every house. The other one, the conveyance or transfer, is dealt with in the next chapter and does not always need to be signed by the buyer.

The exact contents of a contract vary, but it always contains:

the name of the seller and the capacity in which he sells (as trustee, or as owner, or as executor);

the name of the buyer;

a description of the property (often couched in the florid language used in conveyances: ALL THAT freehold land situate at Bursledon in the County of Hants with the dwellinghouse and garage thereon known as 14 Chestnut Avenue Bursledon aforesaid as the same are shown on the plan annexed hereto and thereon coloured pink and brown);

the price and amount of deposit and probably also a statement whether it is to be held as stakeholders or as agents for the vendor;

the date for completing the purchase;

whether the property is freehold or leasehold. The title of a house should be freehold or a long lease; for a flat or maisonette you want a long lease. Anything else needs careful thought and advice; see a solicitor immediately you know the length of the lease offered to you.

Registered or Unregistered?

The contract also states whether the title to the land is registered or unregistered. Land registration was introduced to simplify the buying and selling of houses. Every outright owner without a mortgage on his house has an official land certificate, containing the address of the land, its position on the map, the owner's name and address, and details of special conditions affecting the land. If there is a mortgage, a similar certificate is issued, this time to the lender. A copy of the mortgage is usually bound up with the certificate, which is now known as a charge certificate. Copies of land certificates and charge certificates are available to owners and to their solicitors, and are constantly brought up to date. It is a good system and it is a pity it is spreading so slowly.

Registration of land (although it goes back even further) was generally introduced by the Land Registration Act of 1925, which gave local authorities power to introduce compulsory registration in their area. All land sold after the introduction of compulsory registration has to be put on the Land Register. Virtually all houses in areas such as London, Middlesex, Hastings and Eastbourne are registered, but there are parts of the country which do not yet have compulsory registration, and many more which introduced the system only a few years ago. In those areas, for example Brighton (which introduced compulsory registration in 1965), Bolton (1965), Altrincham (1974) and Manchester (1961), houses have to be registered on the first sale after the system came into force.

All council houses sold under the Housing Act 1980 must be registered even if they are not in a compulsory area. This should give the buyer additional protection: local authority titles are not always clear and straightforward.

Finally, there are the 'Conditions of Sale'. A great many of these, like the rules of cricket or tennis, are there to be referred to if certain contingencies arise. They are laid down once and for all and need not be repeated in every contract any more than the rules of play need to be read out at the start of every game. The contract will say something like: 'The property is sold subject to the National Conditions of Sale which shall be deemed to be incorporated in this contract so far as they are not inconsistent with the conditions herein contained.' One condition frequently changed relates to the rate of interest you will have to pay if you don't produce the purchase money on the date fixed for completion.

The contract is usually prepared in duplicate, one copy signed by the vendor, the other by the purchaser. Payment of the 10 per cent deposit and the exchange of the two copies – the seller's with the buyer's – fixes the point of no return. Once contracts are exchanged you are bound in law to go on with your purchase, and the seller is bound to go on with the sale. This is so whether you live or die, whether the house is burnt down and whether you get your mortgage or not. You now know why so much time and effort and heart-searching are required before a contract is signed.

By the time you come to sign the contract you ought to know:

what the local authority has in store for your house;
any unusual disclosures made by the present owner;
how much money the building society (or other lender) will lend;
whether you have enough to pay the deposit and the balance;
whether you can afford to run the house;
what your surveyor says about it.

Sign only when you are satisfied on all these points.

Chapter 13

Between Contract and Completion

Do not be surprised if you find that you are more than usually irritable shortly after deciding to buy a house. You will worry about whether the owner is likely to sell to somebody else and will be impatient to get contracts exchanged. You will also worry about your chances of getting a mortgage. At the same time you will almost certainly like the house less well on your second visit than on your first, you may have a surveyor's report showing that it is far from perfect, and you may wonder whether it is worth sinking so much money in it. These are anxious days, but if you put yourself in the hands of a good solicitor and a good surveyor you should come through safely.

Once you have made the momentous decision and have exchanged contracts, the air clears. You are now in a similar position to the man who is engaged to be married: he does not at this stage have a wife, and you do not have a house, but both of you have taken on some of the responsibilities of your future state. Unlike an engagement, however, the exchange of contracts on a house tends to take place in the absence of those chiefly affected. The contract is typed out in duplicate, you sign one copy and the seller signs the other. You give yours to your solicitor with the 10 per cent deposit, and carry on with something else. He sends contract and deposit to the seller's solicitor, who in exchange sends the copy signed by his client.

Contracts are 'exchanged' at the precise point when the seller's copy is posted to the buyer's solicitor. From that time onwards both sides are bound. What is more, the house is now formally yours, though you have no right to occupy it till you have paid the balance of the purchase price.

As the house is yours, the seller has to take good care of your property. If he breaks a window, or backs his car into the garden fence, he has to mend it. You, on the other hand, will suffer if the house burns down, if a burglar breaks the windows or a storm takes off the roof. You will nevertheless have to go on with your purchase. This is why your solicitor insures the house as a matter of course as soon as contracts are exchanged. When there is a mortgage, the lender usually insists on handling the insurance though you can suggest an insurance company. Most people take out a comprehensive insurance policy, and many building societies insist on this, though a few are satisfied if you insure against fire risk only.

House Insurance

If you have a choice it is worth shopping around: some policies are slightly more 'comprehensive' than others, and some companies offer a 'no claims bonus' in the form of a free renewal every sixth year if there have been no claims during the previous five years.

A comprehensive policy should include insurance against loss or damage caused by:

fire, explosion, lightning, earthquake and subsidence;
all types of theft;
storms, burst pipes and leaking fuel tanks or washing machines;
aeroplanes or cars (other than your own) crashing into the building;
broken washbasins or fixed glass;
damage to underground cables and pipes;
architects', surveyors' and legal fees (see over);
removal of debris;
injury or damage to strangers (e.g. from a falling roof tile).

Most policies, though including storm damage and damage caused by water, make the onwer bear the first portion of expense. For an extra premium that limit can be removed.

The fact that architects' fees etc. are included may reassure you rather more than it ought to. Imagine that the house is totally destroyed by fire: the most the insurance company would pay is the amount for which you have insured. Out of this you would have to remove debris, redesign and rebuild the house. It is therefore wise to add 15 per cent to the amount for which you would otherwise insure. Some companies, to make this difficulty clear, offer architects' fees etc. as an additional insurance.

How much to insure for? With an average house you won't go far wrong if you insure for about the amount you pay for the house. If you are buying at a bargain price, you may wish to insure for rather more. In any event, review the insurance every few years. It should always be high enough for the house to be completely rebuilt in case of disaster. To allow for the rise in building costs your insurance company may well automatically increase the sum insured each year. If not, remember to check when you get your premium demand: how much are you insured for? Some building societies collect house insurance premiums once a year; others spread premiums over the whole year – adding one twelfth to each monthly mortgage demand. If yours does this, it is easy to forget to check from time to time how much you are insured for. Building societies insist on a minimum insurance cover, but you yourself can always go higher.

While I am dealing with the gloomy side: what would happen to your house if the owner or a member of his family died before completion? The sale would have to go on, however inconvenient this might be for the survivors. Your contract, once made, does not depend on the owner living to complete the sale. If the owner died you would have to wait until someone took out the papers needed to confirm him in the office of personal representative and you would then buy the house from him.

Nor does the purchaser's death end a contract to buy a house. Anyone who is buying with the aid of an endowment policy would therefore do well to take out the policy as soon as contracts are exchanged. The policy would mature on the death of the purchaser and would provide the purchase money. And of course the house could always be resold if it were no longer suitable for the buyer's family.

For those borrowing money under a repayment mortgage, a mortgage protection policy is useful, particularly for the family man.

Even if there is no insurance policy there is a way out. This is what happened in Laura Piper's family: her brother George was killed in a car crash two days after signing the contract for a new house. George's widow could not afford the house. She put it into the hands of estate agents who found another buyer for the house. Through her solicitor she applied for probate of George's will and after a few weeks she sold the house as his executor without losing too much money over it.

Legal Documents

The Title Deeds

Your solicitors will have a copy of the entries on the Land Register affecting your new house (pages 147–9) and an authority to inspect the original. Armed with these two documents, your solicitors can check whether the copy is accurate and whether it refers to the same house and the same owner as the contract, and can make sure that there are no restrictions of which they were not told before, and that the present owner's mortgage will be paid off before you take over ownership.

Not every investigation of title, even of registered land, is so simple. Where there is, for example, a new housing estate with leases to each new owner, or a sale by an executor, or a sale of a small portion of a large estate, the documents can be voluminous and awkward to examine. This is your solicitor's problem, not yours, but it may have some influence on the fees you have to pay.

When the title is not registered, there is every chance that the documents, even in a simple case, will be lengthy and numerous.

You are entitled to know the continuous history of the house: who sold it to whom and for how much, who took it on whose death, whether it was mortgaged and if every mortgage was paid off. To find out, your solicitor goes through the title deeds for at least the last fifteen years. One of the points he checks is whether you are getting the right house. This is quite easy if the house has always been known by the same number and the street by the same name. But in our once rural country this cannot be taken for granted. Many years ago a piece of rural England, part of a county largely owned by one of the big landowning families, was charged with providing pin money for one of the daughters on her marriage. Later she released some of that land to her youngest son, who exchanged it for another piece of land belonging to his elder brother. True to the highest family traditions both brothers had long and almost identical names. One brother went on farming the land and left it to his son, who left it to his own son who used some of the land to pay death duties and sold the rest to a builder. The other brother went mad, his land had to be looked after by someone else and sold as the need arose. Some of it was sold to the same builder, who eventually sold part of his land to another builder who put up twenty-seven semi-detached houses.

If you are buying a semi-detached house, you want to be sure it is one of the twenty-seven and not a house wrongfully built on land belonging to someone else. Investigating a title of this sort is detective work. Similar problems may be involved in checking the credentials of the seller. Is he the owner of the house? If not, how did he acquire the right to sell? He may be the owner's executor – in which case all is well – or he may be a confidence trickster – in which case it is not.

In the course of investigating the title your solicitor will probably fire another list of questions at the vendor's solicitor. These are called 'Requisitions on Title' and are aimed at clearing up all doubts which may arise on investigating the title deeds. At the same time he will also find out where the sale is going to be completed and what banker's drafts will be needed (more about both these below).

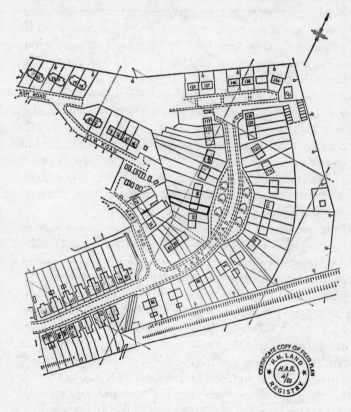

(Reproduced by kind permission of the Chief Land Registrar)

H.M. LAND REGISTRY

A. PROPERTY REGISTER

containing the description of the registered land and the estate comprised in the Title

COUNTY	DISTRICT
BLANKSHIRE	BROXMORE

The Freehold land shown and edged with red on the plan of the above Title filed at the Registry registered on 14 April 1980 known as 95 Cabot Road.

B. PROPRIETORSHIP REGISTER

stating nature of the Title, name, address and description of the proprietor of the land and any entries affecting the right of disposing thereof

TITLE ABSOLUTE

Entry number	Proprietor, etc.
1.	MICHAEL BENNETT Plumber and MARY SUSAN BENNETT his wife both of 95 Cabot Road, Broxmore, Blankshire, registered on 14 April 1980.
2.	RESTRICTION registered on 14 April 1980. No disposition by one proprietor of the land (being the survivor of joint proprietors and not being a trust corporation) under which capital money arises is to be registered except under an order of the registrar or of the Court.

Demand No. 803744011/79 W & W Ltd. 1314

Register Model III   *Any entries struck through are no longer subsisting*

C. CHARGES REGISTER

containing charges, incumbrances etc., adversely affecting the land and registered dealings therewith

Entry number	The date at the beginning of each entry is the date on which the entry was made on this edition of the register	Remarks
1.	14 April 1980—A Conveyance dated 30 September 1934 and made between (1) Mary Brown (Vendor) and (2) Harold Robins (Purchaser) contains the following covenants:— "The Purchaser hereby covenants with the Vendor for the benefit of her adjoining land known as 85, 87, 89, 91 and 93 Cabot Road to observe and perform the stipulations and conditions contained in the Schedule hereto:— THE SCHEDULE before referred to 1. No building to be erected on the land shall be used other than as a private dwellinghouse. 2. No building to be erected as aforesaid shall be converted into or used as flats, maisonettes or separate tenements or as a boarding house. 3. The garden ground of the premises shall at all times be kept in neat and proper order and condition and shall not be converted to any other use whatsoever. 4. Nothing shall be done or permitted on the premises which may be a nuisance or annoyance to the adjoining houses or to the neighbourhood."	
2.	14 April 1980—CHARGE dated 2 April 1980 registered on 14 April 1980 to secure the moneys including the further advances therein mentioned.	
3.	PROPRIETOR—BLANKSHIRE BUILDING SOCIETY of 27 High Street, Broxmore, Blankshire, registered on 14 April 1980.	

Any entries struck through are no longer subsisting

Form 19(JP)

IIM Land Registry   Land Registration Acts, 1925 to 1971

Stamp pursuant to section 28 of the Finance Act 1931 to be impressed here	When the transfer attracts Inland Revenue duty, the stamps should be impressed here before lodging the transfer for registration

(1) For a transfer to a sole proprietor use printed form 19.

(¹) TRANSFER OF WHOLE TO JOINT PROPRIETORS
(Freehold or Leasehold)
(Rules 98 or 115, Land Registration Rules 1925)

County and district }   Blankshire, Broxmore
(or London borough)

Title number(s)   BLK0009

Property   95 Cabot Road

Date................................19...... In consideration of ....TWENTY-EIGHT THOUSAND ----

(2) Strike out if not required.

---------------------pounds (£ 28,000.00---------) (²)*the receipt whereof is hereby acknowledged*

(3) In BLOCK LETTERS, enter full name(s), postal address(es) and occupation(s) of the proprietor(s) of the land.

(³)I/We Michael Bennett and Mary Susan Bennett both of 95 Cabot Road,

Broxmore, Blankshire

(4) If desired, or otherwise as the case may be (see rules 76 and 77).

(⁴)*as beneficial owner(s)* hereby transfer to:

(5) In BLOCK LETTERS, enter full name(s), postal address(es) and occupation(s) of the transferee(s) for entry on the register.

(⁵)

Thomas Alexander Jones and May Jones both of 10 Mildert Walk, Durham

(6) Any special clause should be entered here.

(7) A transfer for charitable uses should follow form 36 (see rules 121 and 122).

the land comprised in the title(s) above mentioned (⁶) (⁷)

(continued overleaf)

The Transfer or Conveyance

When he is satisfied about the title, your solicitor prepares the document which will transfer the ownership of the house from its present owner to you. As a general rule a conveyance (of unregistered land) (see page 152) is a more complex document than a transfer (of registered) (see above).

When more than one person is buying, the words 'as beneficial

Conveyances of unregistered land follow a set pattern. After the names and addresses of seller and buyer, the part beginning WHEREAS ... tells of any important events which have happened since the last conveyance – in the present case very little. Had the last owner died, this would be recounted here with the name of his executor and the date of probate and would explain why the executor rather than the last owner was selling.

NOW THIS DEED ... signifies the beginning of the conveyance proper: first, the price, then whether the owner sells his own or somebody else's property, next a description of what he is selling.

TO HOLD starts the part showing whether the buyer is getting freehold or leasehold ('in fee simple' means he is buying freehold) and whether there are any special rules affecting the house. These are the 'restrictions and stipulations contained in the ... Conveyance'. They might say, for example, that the house was to be used only as a private residence and not for business, or that no washing must be put out on Sundays.

The conveyance will be shown to Smith's solicitor in draft; he may suggest alterations, and after the draft has been agreed between solicitors and typed on very strong paper or parchment (it will have to last for many years), it is sent to John Smith to sign in the presence of a witness. After John Smith has signed, the last clause looks like this:

SIGNED SEALED AND DELIVERED by
the said JOHN SMITH in the   } *J. Smith*   ●
presence of:

T. Hubbard

2 The Crossroads
Sarisbury, Hants
Engineer

A small red wafer seal will be stuck to the right of Mr Smith's signature. There is no magic about these positions, but they make for order, just as it does if long stop knows that he stands behind the wicket keeper. In the simplest cases the buyer need not sign the transfer or conveyance; they are signed merely by the seller. A mortgage, on the other hand, always needs the signature of the borrower.

Mortgages

Mortgages tend to be long and complicated. Some typical clauses are set out in Chapter 3, 'Where Will the Money Come From?' The points of importance to the house-buyer (in the mortgage he is called 'the Borrower') are the amount of his monthly or quarterly payments, and the knowledge that the mortgage gives the lender formidable powers to enforce regular payment. In the last resort a lender can sell a house over a defaulting borrower's head. What is more, this happens after the borrower has been taken to court, at his own expense.

Within a few days of completing the house purchase you will be told the day of the month when your mortgage payments are due. It is a good idea to arrange with your bank to pay the mortgage each month by banker's order or direct debit. This avoids the risk of the payment being overlooked. The bank, of course, can pay only if there is enough money in your account: whatever else you have to cut down on, be sure to keep the account healthy. If you have arranged for direct debit payments, remember when the building society told you they would go up. Even the most careful plans can be upset by illness, unemployment or divorce. Here are some hints which may help should you strike unlucky:

(1) Tell the mortgagees what has happened and ask whether for a limited time they will let you pay less. Building societies are often prepared to let you pay the interest only, and not to make repayments of capital. Even these payments may be high, but every little will help.

(2) If you are out of work for a long time, allow your capital

(excluding the house) to drop below £3,000 and apply for supplementary benefit. The Department of Health and Social Security, though it does not pay endowment premiums, can probably help pay the mortgage interest.

(3) If the drop in income is permanent (for example, your wife may stop work to have a baby), ask the building society whether they will extend the mortgage (say, from twenty-five to thirty years), thus reducing your monthly payments.

(4) Building societies much prefer their mortgage money to remain in your house, rather than get a bad name for making people homeless when they fall on hard times. Be open with your building society and you will find them understanding. What you must avoid at all cost is to fall behind, without explanation, in the forlorn hope that they will not notice. They always do.

Chapter 14

Preparing Your Move

The contract usually fixes a date for completion, about four weeks ahead, to give everyone time to make final arrangements.

You and the Seller

Once contracts have been exchanged, sellers – even those who previously kept you very much at arm's length – usually become friendly and helpful. You may get useful information about school, church, doctor, butcher, newspaper shop and others.

Settle with the owner whether gas, electricity and water are or are not to be cut off. In winter it is wise to turn off water at the mains if the house is to be unoccupied for even a short period. If you move in on the day he moves out, much trouble can be saved by leaving all supplies connected. In that case sign agreements with the Gas and Electricity Boards before you move in, but make it clear that you will move – and be responsible for supplies – on, say, the 15th and not before. Remind the owner to have his meter read before he leaves. You may also be able to take over his telephone.

The seller is, up to the date of the sale, responsible for all the outgoings on the house from rates to newspapers. It is up to him to cancel milk, electricity, etc., and for you, the buyer, to arrange your own supplies.

The Seller and His Solicitor

Rates, water rates and ground rent continue, whoever owns the house. But the old owner does not have to pay the new man's rates. He could ask the council for a refund, but often his solicitor, to save him trouble, works out exactly how much is due by the old owner and how much by the new, and adjusts the figure on completion. If the old owner has paid beyond the date of sale, he gets a proportion back; if it is the other way round, he either pays, or makes an allowance on completion.

Whatever method is used, the new owner is responsible for rates and water rates from completion of the purchase. If you are not moving in for some time after buying, tell the council, because you may not have to pay rates while the house is empty.

Apart from rates (and ground rent and insurance in a leasehold house or flat) the seller's solicitors find out from his building society exactly how much is needed to repay his mortgage on the completion date. This is repaid when you buy the house, and you are not concerned with it.

After this the vendor's solicitor prepares a 'completion statement' and sends it to your solicitor. A traditional completion statement looks something like this:

re 14 Chestnut Avenue, Bursledon
Completion statement as at 1st May 19..

Purchase price	£30,000·00	
Less deposit already paid	£3,000·00	
	£27,000·00	
Deduct proportion of General Rate		
1·4 to 30·4 (30 days)		
at £400 per year		£32·87
		£26,967·13

(This means that the vendor has paid rates up to 31 March, but not beyond.)

Add proportion of water rate
  1·5 to 30·6 (61 days)
  at £36 per year   £6·02

Amount payable on completion   £26,973·15

(*Vendor has paid water rate in advance and gets back a proportion for the period after the house is no longer his.*)

Please supply two banker's drafts:

£13,194·12 in favour of   (vendor's building society)
£13,779·03 in favour of   (vendor's solicitors)

£26,973·15

Note: Increasingly, solicitors try to obtain apportioned figures direct from the rates department and the Water Board; the result is that the rates will not figure in the amount you pay on completion. Whichever method is used, you are not responsible for the old owner's rate or water rate. Your responsibility starts when you become the owner of the house.

Your Solicitors (1)

At this stage, your solicitors will:

  check the completion statement for errors of addition;
  prepare their bill of costs and send it to you;
  find out exactly how much money your building society will provide on completion, after allowing for stamp duties, legal fees, a copy of the mortgage, guarantee policy premium, retention for repairs, final inspection fee, etc. – these vary from case to case.

When they have all the figures, they send you a statement explaining how much they need from you. They will want the amount on the completion statement, plus their costs, stamp duties, Land Registry fees, etc. less the amount which will come from the building society. They will also tell you whether they need a cheque or a banker's draft from you.

You (1)

You will probably have to visit your solicitors to sign the mortgage, possibly also the conveyance or transfer.

If they tell you that the conveyance or transfer needs your signature, do not delay. You will have to sign before the seller can sign, so get the document back into the hands of your solicitors as quickly as possible.

If you think you are likely to be away when all this is happening, it is a good idea to give your solicitors plenty of warning.

If you get mortgage or conveyance or transfer through the post, do make a point of signing where you are asked to sign. The buyer usually signs to the right of the small clause which starts: SIGNED ... and contains his name. The witness to the signature signs underneath that clause, adding his address and occupation after his signature. You don't (see p. 152). One or two building societies, to show how thoroughly modern they are, have reversed the order. The borrower signs on the left, the witness on the right – both on the same line. One good look at the end of the mortgage will tell what is expected of you.

Remember that a cheque may need up to ten days to be cleared, so be sure to send the money in good time to your solicitors.

If there is not enough time, your solicitor will ask you for a banker's draft – a glorified cheque, signed by the bank manager. To get a banker's draft, you draw a cheque on your own bank, hand it to the branch where you keep your account, and ask the bank to make out a banker's draft. This takes only a few minutes. The bank will charge a small fee.

Your Solicitors (2)

A few days before completion, your solicitors make a search at the Land Registry or the Land Charges Registry.

The Land Registry search is a simple and effective check on

whether anyone is trying to doublecross you, and makes sure that
the house is not going to be sold to two people at once. If the search
is clear, it not only reassures you that no one has tried to snatch
ownership from you, it goes further and promises that for fourteen
working days from the date of your search the Land Registry will
not deal with anyone else. This gives your solicitors time to complete the purchase, stamp the papers and lodge them with the
Registry, who then put your name on the Register as that of the
new owner. No one else has a chance of dishonestly slipping in.
For a house with unregistered title a similar search is made at the
Land Charges Registry. The solicitors acting for your building
society will also make a search to find out whether you have gone
bankrupt. If you have, you will not get your mortgage.

With luck your solicitors will, on the day before completion,
have the completion money from the building society and from
you, cleared and available to draw against. The completion statement tells them whether the purchase money is to be paid in one
sum to the seller's solicitors or partly to them and partly to the
seller's building society. As soon as all the money is in their hands,
your solicitors finalize the completion of your purchase, either by
transferring the money to the seller's solicitors' bank or by going
to their office armed with banker's drafts.

Chains

Not what they use to stop you from committing murder if you can't
get into your new house on the due date. We talk of chains when
several people have to buy and sell their houses on the same day.
You cannot buy your new house and move in till you have the
money for your old house. The man who is buying your old house
cannot do so till he has been paid by the people who are buying
his. And so on … If there is a breakdown somewhere, a large
number of people can be in trouble.

There are those who blame the solicitors and sit back in anger.
More realistically, you can plan for such emergencies and go on

hoping they will not happen. Miraculously, the majority of completions take place on the intended day.

How to Cope with Delay

Obviously you will do all you can to avoid delay. Make sure your solicitor knows where to get hold of you, that you know how much money is needed from you, and get the right amount into the hands of your solicitor in time. Problems sometimes arise because documents get lost or are delayed in the post. It is hoped that local authorities, land registries and building societies will soon all communicate with solicitors by computer and that this will simplify the procedure somewhat. Keep your fingers crossed! When the computer breaks down, we shall no doubt bemoan the good old days when letters, more often than not, reached their proper destination.

Emergency No. 1: You Cannot Get into Your New House

The most likely cause of trouble is money: someone along the line does not have enough money to complete on time. If your seller cannot move to his new house he may decide to stay put, and you cannot move into his old one. You can either react by also staying put, or, if you have planned ahead, move in with friends or relations for a few days. If you yourself make it clear that you are ready to complete your purchase, you will neither pay interest to your seller for late completion, nor will you start paying interest on your new mortgage if the delay is at all prolonged. Unfortunately, the seller will not owe you compensation either unless the delay is so long that completion notices have been served. At the same time, by moving out and completing the sale of your old house you will have paid off your old mortgage and will have a large sum of money in the bank.

Emergency No. 2: You Cannot Complete Your own Purchase on Time

Here again, the most likely reason is money: your mortgage cheque or your own cheque for the balance has not been cleared, or your buyer has been held up. If this cannot be overcome in a day, the quickest solution probably is a bridging loan from your bank. Weigh up the cost of such a loan against the inconvenience of changing your plans and the cost of completing late. This cost depends on how much interest you save on *not* taking out your new mortgage and how much interest you have to pay for not buying on the date fixed for completion. Your solicitors can help with the calculations. At present, delayed completion is more expensive for the frustrated buyer than for the seller, who has at least a fortnight's grace. There is a move afoot to make sellers, too, pay compensation to the buyer for every day's delay caused by them. It will depend on the state of the housing market whether the idea catches on.

Moving Before Completion

It is usually a term of the contract that 'vacant possession shall be given on completion', which means that the purchaser gets the key to the house against his purchase money. Occasionally, the old owner moves out before completion and, rather than leave the house empty, allows the new owner to move in before the purchase money is ready. This seemingly simple courtesy can have serious legal results for the seller. Do not, therefore, consider him unreasonable if, after taking advice from his solicitor, he says No to a request to move in early.

However, some owners will allow purchasers in. Usually this is on terms that the buyer pays rates and other outgoings from the time he moves in, and that he pays interest on the purchase money.

It is often as cheap to borrow money and to complete earlier, or to store your furniture and stay with your in-laws for a month.

If you are lucky, the old owner may allow you to prepare your move some days ahead, without your having to pay. He may let you do repairs, or start painting, so long as you give him your word not to move in before the completion date.

Or, you may have a few days after completion while the new home is being cleaned up, carpets are fitted, alterations put in hand. But far more often everything has to be done on one day: you arrive, put down floor tiles and carpets as you go along, swiftly, so that the heavy pieces of furniture can come next and you can start emptying boxes and filling cupboards. Such a move repays careful preparation.

You (2): Preparing Your Move

Removal costs vary; it is worth getting several estimates. As well as comparing prices, try to get a personal recommendation. Some removers are very much more skilful, quick and considerate than others.

If you are moving to or from a big city, you often do better to look for a remover in the smaller place. Thus, for example, many firms have loads to go to London and but for your move might have to return empty. They will probably charge less for the move than a London firm. Also, move in the middle of the week, in the middle of the month, if you can. Removal firms get very busy on Fridays and at the beginning and end of the month. Take off, say, Thursday, to move. Ignore the mess while you are at work on Friday and spend the weekend getting settled. It is less exhausting and probably cheaper.

You don't necessarily save money by doing your own packing – ask the removal firm about this. Alternatively, go the whole hog and tackle the move yourself (see p. 168 for the grisly experience of the author). To do this, you need (1) a van; (2) a driver with the appropriate driving licence; (3) able-bodied and skilful helpers.

A small (30 cwt) van is useful for a move over a short distance; you can move one or two rooms at a time. For longer distances, several journeys are expensive and time-consuming. Bear in mind, though, that to drive a large van you need an HGV licence.

Make sure that the driver can handle a van and that both driver and furniture are insured as far as possible. If you are able to borrow the van from a friend, check both his and your own car insurance – one or other may well cover the van. If you hire a van, check with the hire company.

If you hire a van, it is a good idea to pick it up early enough for a trial run. A van in bad shape can literally throw a spanner in the works. You need all your time and energy for the move and have none to spare trying to repair a van that has not been overhauled before you receive it.

The move will go considerably more smoothly if you have taken care of certain things beforehand.

Furniture insurance: Tell your insurance company when you intend to move and ask them to insure your chattels during the removal and at your new address. If you want to change insurance companies, this is a good moment: tell the old one to cancel your policy as from the day after you leave and to refund the rest of the year's premium. Ask the new company to insure the furniture in transit and at the new house.

Gas and electricity: Unless your new house is going to be all electric, write to both Area Boards asking them to lay on supplies. When the moving day has been fixed, arrange for the Board to send a fitter to the new house, to connect the cooker on that day. Also arrange for your own cooker to be disconnected and your meters to be read. Give the Board as much notice as you can. They often find it unbelievably difficult to disconnect and reconnect a cooker on one and the same day.

Telephone: It is easy to have your old telephone cut off, but it can be difficult and frustratingly slow to get a telephone in your new home. Try to take over the seller's telephone; installing a new one is expensive and often takes time. Some telephone managers, far from eager to do business, convey the impression that you are being greedy and unreasonable in wanting a telephone ready and functioning when you move in. Do not be disheartened but do allow time for making arrangements.

Letters: Arrange for the Post Office to forward them to your new address. The Post Office will supply a form for you to fill in and return.

Tell your friends: To be on the safe side, send your change of address to friends, bank, etc. – to anyone whose letters you value.

School: If the move means a change of school for your children, do not forget to tell the new Education Authority when they will be starting.

Food: Even if there is not time for a visit to the area, try to find out where the nearest shops are. Perhaps the seller will lay on milk at least for the first day.

Keys: Persuade the owner to leave all his keys when he moves out, and arrange where to pick them up. The most convenient method is to leave one key with the estate agent, if he is nearby, or with a neighbour. The remaining keys are often left on the mantelpiece. You are not entitled to a key till you have completed the purchase.

Most important: Arrange who is to be where on moving day. Your children will probably have the day off school, but anyone under fifteen is likely to get weary long before the move is complete. (So, for that matter, will you, but bear up, you don't have to move every day.) Overrule the children's protests and arrange for them to spend the day with some fond relation. If possible, let them take all pets; this has the double merit of keeping the pets out of the way and stopping the children from feeling unwanted.

Before you usher them out, ask the children to prepare number cards, one for each room in the new house. Also lay in a box of drawing pins or sticky tack and a piece of chalk. Give each room in the new house a number, and mark each piece of furniture and every heavy box or trunk with the number. This prevents grand-father's bed from landing up in the nursery while your back is turned.

Moving Day

Do not have too many helpers. The ideal number is three to four: two knowledgeable members of your household and one friend or possibly two, experienced in moving house. Try to have one knowledgeable member of the household in the old house and one in the new to deal with unforeseen queries. No move is without them: do the goldfish stay in the pond or come with you? What happens to the pelmets, or dustbins? What about the suit still at the dry cleaner's, and the card for Aunt Lucy's eightieth birthday on the mantelpiece? A helpful stranger might post it, not knowing that the card had been written a year earlier and the old lady had passed away in the meantime.

While you are waiting for the removal van, you will have time for a last nostalgic look round the house. Check whether you have marked all pieces of furniture with room numbers for the new house. Keep some spare chalk to mark the chests which the removal men will bring for china, etc. Do not trouble to pack china or glass, unless you are convinced that you are better at packing than they are. They will come armed with tea chests and packing material.

Removers have an uncanny knack of taking apart large pieces of furniture, such as wardrobes and cupboards. For this reason, clothes as well as sweaters and shoes and other articles kept on shelves inside your wardrobe usually travel better in trunks. Stuff kept in drawers, on the other hand, can travel without being shifted.

The contents of drawers in fitted cupboards are easily forgotten, so are things in the attic, garden, outhouses and anywhere above eye level. This is where an experienced member of the household can prove his mettle. He will also make sure that you leave behind all the bits and pieces which you have sold, or promised to leave for the new owner.

The other experienced member will have found out where the nearest phone box is, and made sure that there will be parking space for the removal van outside the new house. He will, if possible, arrive ahead of the van, taking with him:

(1) the numbered cards and drawing pins or sticky tape. He will fix one to each door. If he is at all absent-minded, or if the house has many rooms, give him a plan showing which room is to have what number, otherwise the piano may yet turn up in the bedroom and the wardrobe in the dining room;

(2) a broom, bucket and rough cleaning materials. Even if the house is left beautifully clean, he (or more likely she) will feel less lonely if she can do some cleaning while she waits for the removal van;

(3) a toilet roll, towel and soap;

(4) a number of coins for telephoning, even if you have arranged to take over the telephone in the house. Telephones have been known to break down;

(5) a camping stove if you have, or can borrow, one, with a kettle, several mugs and all that is needed for morale-raising cups of tea while you are waiting. Indeed you might as well play safe and allow for the cooker not being reconnected on the day of your move. This can be borne more equably if your family is not on a strict diet of exclusively cold food.

The experienced member will check whether the seller has left behind all the things included in the sale, and will rejoice in any she finds without having to pay for them. Many owners abandon lino and vinyl (they move very badly), curtain rails and light fittings. But should you find lampshades or lawn mowers it would be better to put them on one side and find out whether the seller meant to leave them or merely forgot them. You will probably have asked for his new address – you are bound to get letters addressed to him even if he made arrangements with the Post Office.

Once the removal men arrive things tend to move swiftly. Before long the floor will be littered with shoes, books, washing-up mops, light bulbs, blankets and cat food. Workmen who swore they could not fit you in for a fortnight will appear; so will goods which you may or may not have ordered.

Do-It-Yourself Move

In our family we can muster six able-bodied adults and are blessed with practical and helpful friends: we have recently tackled several moves which, though exhausting, were also quite fun and the occasion for a family reunion. We none of us have an HGV licence, nor have we tackled long-distance moves. Whoever comes furthest usually brings the hired van, saving his rail fare. To get a good van we have found a matter of trial and error. If you cannot get a personal recommendation, the Yellow Pages in your telephone directory are as good a guide as any. Most firms give a choice between a daily all-in charge, and a lower charge plus so much per mile. For short-distance moves, it is usually cheaper to pay mileage.

For about a fortnight before the move we collect cardboard boxes from our supermarket and fill them up gradually. We have learnt the hard way that very large boxes may be suitable for large quantities of cornflakes but will collapse if filled with clothes, books or china. Middle-sized boxes are best. We pack every piece of glass and china separately in newspaper. This is a bore and takes up a lot of time and space. But we have never yet broken anything.

Hi-fi equipment, records and delicate glass, etc., do of course prefer the back seat of a car to any van, however carefully driven. If time allows, two of us have decorated at least the main living room before the big move. Very often, of course, time does not allow, and everything has to be done in one day. In that case two of us start cleaning up and, with luck, painting one room as soon as we can get into the new house.

The movers at the old house must remember to start by loading the light articles and end up with the heavy ones, leaving the carpet until the end. If you move one room at a time, this happens almost automatically. When you arrive at the new house, you want the carpet out first, next you want to get at the sideboard without having to lift a lot of boxes off first. Some of the furniture will have been taken to pieces – this is fine if you are good at jigsaw puzzles and have a strong nerve. I have neither and usually panic at this stage. A chorus of 'Don't worry' sends me off to make a cup of tea for everyone.

One helper will in any event spend most of the day preparing and clearing away meals, plus cleaning and putting stuff away in cupboards. We have found it a good idea to concentrate on getting one, or possibly two, rooms into a reasonable state by the evening. One habitable room in contrast with others in a state of chaos makes us feel much better than several rooms all vaguely coming along. When you sit down to your well-deserved evening meal it also helps if you have made sure of a bed for the night. Well, if not a bed, at least a mattress; and if not a mattress, some clear floor space and a blanket.

One ray of light: you do not have to concern yourself with the completion of the house purchase. This is in the hands of your solicitors and of the other lawyers involved: an ordinary completion may need as many as four.

The Solicitors

Traditionally, all completions are attended personally. At the time fixed for completion several solicitors or their clerks detach themselves from their work and turn up at the office of the solicitor for the seller's building society. Your solicitor arrives armed with your contribution to the purchase money, and with the mortgage which you signed a few days earlier. Your building society's solicitor arrives with the building society money, and both solicitors have a look at the title deeds to make sure that all is well – this is your solicitor's last chance of seeing them because the deeds will be kept by your building society till you have repaid every penny of the mortgage. Your solicitor also looks at the rate receipts – these will be produced by the seller's solicitor – to make sure that the rates have been paid up to date; and he looks at the conveyance or transfer to see that it has been properly signed. This vital document forms part of the title deeds and goes to your building society. Here again, unless your solicitor also acts for the building society, this is his only chance of seeing it. Your solicitor gives the seller's solicitor the banker's draft he has brought with him and everyone starts adding busily to see whether the money provided by building society A plus the draft provided by you comes to the amount needed to repay building society B plus the balance in the completion statement. It usually does, and everyone heaves a sigh of relief.

Completions are even more involved if you are selling one house and buying another, all on the same day; they become almost impossible when money has to be gathered in one town and paid out in another. Modern practice often follows a different pattern from the traditional one. Completions are often effected through the post or by bank transfer. It still seems to require considerable effort by banks to get money transferred within a working day. With any luck, however, this is quicker than a solicitor travelling to Manchester, clutching a banker's draft. Bank transfers also make it possible to cope with a longer chain of completions. But the system depends on very careful preparation and on the bank getting the money transferred quickly.

Surprisingly, solicitors usually manage to get everyone fixed up.

The house key is sometimes handed over on completion, but more often it is left with either an estate agent or with neighbours of the seller; if necessary the seller's solicitor rings up to say it is in order for the key to be handed over to you.

From that moment onwards the house is yours, both in law and in fact.

Glossary of Legal Terms

Banker's Draft	A cheque issued by a bank, accepted instead of cash on completion of sale.
Completion	The exchange of title deeds against balance of purchase money.
Completion Statement	Account of amount payable on completion (purchase price less deposit, plus/minus proportion of rates, ground rent, etc.).
Contract	Agreement between buyer and seller binding both to complete the purchase/sale of the house.
Conveyance	The document which makes the buyer the owner of a house with unregistered title.
Conveyancing	Traditionally, the legal side of buying and selling houses.
	'Conveyancing firm' or 'Conveyancer' are terms that have recently been used to describe the transfer of ownership without legal advice. A government committee is at present (mid 1984) considering whether and on what conditions persons or firms without legal training should be able to act as 'licensed conveyancers'.
Ground Rent	Annual rent paid for a long lease.
Legal charge	Another word for mortgage.
Mortgage	Legal document pledging house as security for a loan.
Mortgagee	Lender of money on the security of a mortgage. Often a building society or bank.
Mortgagor	One who borrows money on mortgage.
Purchaser	The buyer of the house.
Registered Land	Land whose title is registered at H M Land Registry and guaranteed by it.
Restrictive Covenants	Don'ts. Restrictions applying to the use of land.

Title Deeds Documents showing ownership of house.

Transfer The document making the buyer owner of a house with registered title.

Vendor The seller of the house, usually the owner.

Index

Agent for the vendor, deposit to, 100–101, 104
Assignment of NHB Agreement, 62
Auction, buying house by, 124

Banker's draft, 159
Banks, 34
  favourable mortgages for employees, 18, 54
Bridging loan, 104, 136, 162
Budget, 17
Building societies, 34–8
  as lenders, 13, 14–16, 37–8
  favourable mortgages for employees, 18
  inspection fee, 19, 63–4, 106
  methods, 14
  preferences of, 36
  savings, 16, 18, 27, 34–5
  waiting list, 35
Buyer, see Purchaser
Buying by tender, 124

Capital contribution, 59–60
Chains, 160–61
Charge, service, 72
Charge certificates, 140
Completion, 169–70
  date, 134
  moving before, 134, 162–3
  of sale, delay, 161–2
  of sale and purchase, 135–6, 169–70
  payment, 60

statement, 157–8, 160
Conditions of sale, 140–41
Consumer Credit Act 1974, 16
Contract(s)
  contents of, 139–40
  draft, 132
  exchange of, 103, 139–40, 141, 142
  inquiries before, 138–9
  payment, 60
Contribution, capital, 59–60
Conveyance, signing of, 139, 150–54, 159, 169
Conveyancing firms, 61
Co-ownership associations, 127, 128
Costs
  calculation of, 59–74
  general estimates, 163
  solicitors, 60–63
  surveyors, 109, 110
Council houses, 64, 98, 125–6, 140
Council tenant, mortgage, 18

Deeds of covenant, 62
Deeds of variation, 62
Deposit, 17, 19, 99–105
  new houses, 91, 101, 102
  ninety-five per cent mortgage, 104–5
  preliminary, 89, 99–102
  receipt for, 100
  size of, 105
  ten per cent, 103–4
  to house owner direct, 19, 89,

Deposit—*cont.*
  101, 102–3
DHSS, help with mortgage
    payments, 17, 58
Do-it-yourself move, 56, 163–4,
    168–9
Domestic help, 73

Employer, loan by, 54–5
Endowment mortgage, 44–8
  warning, 44
Entertaining, 73
Estate agents, 19, 24–5, 56,
    75–80
  duty to reply, 28
  language of, 76–8
  letter to, 88
  qualifications of, 79–80
Estates, new, mortgages, 18, 24
Exchange of contracts, 103,
    139–40, 141, 142
Executors, buying from, 126

Fares, 72
Fees
  building society inspection, 19,
    63–4, 106
  buyer's solicitor, 60–62, 158
  Land Registry, 64
  legal, 60–63
  minor, 65
  scale of, 63
  stamp duty, 64–5
  survey, 109, 110
Flats, 111–19
  converted, 29–30, 36, 111–12
  described, 29, 78
  lease of, 94, 113, 116, 117
  mortgage for, 29–30, 36–7,
    118–19
  purpose-built, 112–13
  service charge, 72
Freehold, 36, 94–5
Furniture insurance, 70, 164

Gazumping, 90–91

Grant, improvement, 122–3
Ground rent, 69, 94, 117
Guaranteed loan, 52

Home loan, 51–2
Homesteading, 123
House insurance, 69, 143–4
Houses, new, 79, 91, 102,
    119–21
Houses, old, 122–3
Housing Act 1980, 64
Housing associations, 126–8
  co-ownership, 127, 128
  self-build, 127, 128
  shared ownership, 128

Improvement grants, 122–3
Income, building societies' views
    on, 37–8
Index-linked mortgage, 44
Inflation, effect on house prices,
    20
Inquiries before contract, 138–9
Inspection fee, 19, 63–4, 106
Insurance
  endowment, described, 44–8
    warning, 44
  endowment or top up, 70
  furniture, 70, 164
  house, 69, 143–4
  mortgage protection, 42, 56,
    70–71, 145
Insurance brokers, 46, 47, 55
Insurance companies, 34
Interest, 40–41

Joint names, buying in, 134–5
Joint tenants, 135, 150

Land Charges Registry, 65,
    159–60
Land Registry, 62, 64, 65, 140,
    159–60
Lease, new, stamp duty on, 65
Leasehold Reform Act 1967, 36,
    94–5

Leasehold, 36, 94–6, 113
Leaseholder, right to purchase
  freehold, 36
Legal fees, *see* Fees
Letters
  circular, 26
  to an estate agent, 25, 88
  to an owner, 86–8
  to a private advertiser, 25
  to a solicitor, 88–9, 131–2
Loans, 54–5
  home, 51–2
  over £15,000, 48, 49
  private, 54
  top up, 49–50
Local authority
  as lender, 34
  buying council houses, 64, 98,
    125–6
  homesteading scheme, 123
  improvement grant, 122–3
  mortgage, 50–51
  rates, 71, 157
  search, 65, 136–8
Long lease, 36, 94–6
Low cost endowment mortgage,
  45
Low start mortgage, 44, 53–4

Maisonette, 37, 78
Memorandum and Articles, 62
MIRAS, 38–9, 42
Monthly mortgage payments, 38,
  41–2, 68–9
Mortgage, 34–56
  described, 34
  endowment, 44–8
  higher loans, 48
  local authority, 50–51
  low start, 44, 53–4
  one hundred per cent, 53
  payments, 38, 41–2, 68–9
  payments, hard times, 154–5
  protection policy, 42, 56,
    70–71, 145
  repayment mortgage, 40–41

  second, 15, 30, 49–50, 66
  types of, 40–56
  when to apply for, 133–4
  with guarantee policy, 42–3
Mortgage brokers, 15–16
  as lenders, 55, 68
  fee limited by law, 16
  fee recovery difficult, 16
  mortgage facilities, 18
Mortgagee
  described, 34
  solicitor of, 62–3
Mortgagor
  described, 34
Moving, 163–9
Moving date, when to fix, 134

Names, joint, 134–5
New houses, 79, 91, 102,
  119–21
NHBC certificate, 108, 119, 120
Notice to landlord, 134

Old houses, buying, 122–3
  local authority grant for,
    122–3
One hundred per cent mortgage,
  53
Owner
  letter to, 86–8
  not to pay deposit to, 89, 101,
    102–3
Ownership, joint, 134–5

Part possession, 96–7
Payments, mortgage, 38, 41–2,
  68–9
  stage, 120–21
Pension mortgage, 49
Planning permission, 62, 121
Plot, buying a, 121
Policies of Indemnity, 62
Private loan, 54
Property centres, 80
Protection policy, mortgage, 42,
  56, 70–71, 145

Purchaser, 37
  low savings, rising income, 30
  moderate savings, moderate
    income, 29–30
  moving in a hurry, 32–3
  older people, 31–2
  solicitor of, 60–62

Rates, 71, 157, 169
  rateable value, 71
  water, 71, 157
Receipt for deposit, 100
Registered land, 140
  transfer of, 151–2
Registration of land, 140
Removal costs
  estimates, 163
  do-it-yourself, 56, 163–4,
    168–9
Rent acts, 57, 96, 112
Rent, ground, 69, 94, 117
Repairs, 36, 71–2, 106, 122–3
Repayment mortgage, 40–42
Requisitions on title, 146
Retirement, 31
Roads
  maintained at public expense,
    137
  private, 137
  ring, 138
  widening, 137

Savings in building societies, 16,
    18, 27
  as bargaining lever, 34–5
Searches, local authority, 65,
    136–8
  Land Charges Registry, 159,
    160
  Land Registry, 159–60
Second mortgage, 15, 30, 49–50,
    66
Self-build Society, 127, 128
Service charge, 72
Shops, 73
Scale of fees, 63

Shared ownership, 128
Sheltered housing, 31–2
Sitting tennants, 97–8
  mortgage, 18, 53
Smoke control order, 137
Solicitor, 92–8, 131–41
  completion of purchase, 135–6,
    169–70
  information needed by, 133
  letter to, 88–9
  mortgagee's, 62–3
  purchaser's, 56, 60–62,
    158–60
Stage payments, 120–21
Stakeholder, 100, 101, 104
Stamp duty, 64–5, 118
  on new lease, 65
Subject to contract, 87, 101
  Survey fee, 106
  Surveyor, 106–10
  fee, 109, 110
  report, 56, 106, 108–10

Tax relief, on mortgage interest,
    30–31, 33, 38–9
Tenants
  in common, 135, 151
  joint, 135, 151
  sitting, 97–8
Tender, buying by, 124
Thatched cottage, buying, 123
Title
  investigation of, 145–6
  registered and unregistered, 62,
    64, 140
Top up loans, 49–50
  insurance, 70
Transfer of registered land, 150–51

Unit linked mortgage, 48–9

Waiting list, building society, 35
Water rates, 71
Women, mortgages, 37
Woodworm, specialist report,
    107, 108